flippin' chairs

a memoir

Bethany Parks

First Edition
ISBN: 978-0-578-49849-2

Cover design by Teddi Black
Interior design by Megan McCullough
Photograph: Erin Eneboe
Editor: Jennifer Collins

For Mom and Dad.
Forever grateful.

Wednesday, September 24, 2008

Sex. That's what this was all about. I just wanted to have sex.

It was my forty-first birthday and I was perched on an exam table at the gynecologist's office, sporting one of those flimsy blue gowns and scanning an old *People* magazine.

"Hi. I'm Sandy," announced the nurse practitioner as she entered the room and shook my hand.

My filter-less response spewed forth. "Hi. I'm Bethany. I had unprotected sex." An awkward laugh escaped from my throat as the middle-aged nurse with conservative glasses responded with a polite nod of the head.

"You're not alone," she chuckled. "It happens all the time."

I was newly single after seventeen years of marriage, and had made some mistakes. Like the guy I'd been "dating" when I left my marriage. The guy in the well-worn Levis who had the pecs that screamed at me through a tight black T-shirt. The guy with the water-blue eyes and the sense of humor that caught me off-guard every time. The guy who told me I was stronger than I thought I was. He was like a drug to me. He was kindly referred to as "Crack" among my girlfriends.

"I want to do all those tests that responsible people do after they have unprotected sex." It didn't have to be public knowledge that there was another guy waiting in the wings and I had an ulterior motive for this visit.

"Yup. We can do that." Her perfect pixie haircut hung neatly around her doll-like face as she flipped through a manila file and started the obligatory process of making small-talk. "What do you do for a living?"

"I sell furniture. Desks and chairs and conference tables. I work with architects and designers, hospitals and universities."

She responded with the typical response—"Well, that's nice"—and instructed me to slide down and put my feet in the oven mitt-covered stirrups as she snapped on a set of blue latex gloves. The standard OB/GYN exam was underway.

"I'll take the swab for STDs while doing the pap smear," she chirped from behind the blue sheet draped over my knees.

Great. STDs. Forty-one years old and worried about STDs. Were they even called that anymore? Memories of teenage trips to Planned Parenthood ran through my brain. *Protection. Protection. Protection.* I should have asked him to wear a condom. I hated these tests.

"Okey doke!" Sandy smiled as she pulled off the latex gloves. "Slide up and we'll do your breast exam."

Gratefully, I pulled my feet out of the stirrups and scootched up the vinyl bed, trying to regain some sort of dignity.

"Put your right arm over your head." I did as I was told. "So, what type of furniture do you sell?" Sandy's fingers moved in a circular motion around my breast. She pushed under my armpit and around my collarbone as her eyes stared off into space.

"Tables and chairs and conference room furniture. Stuff for offices and waiting rooms and cafeterias and hospitals." Nurses must be trained at making small talk to help distract from these awkward situations. Her fingers made their way around the right side of my chest and back to the area under my collarbone.

"I feel a little lump here," she said, her brow slightly furrowed.

Yeah, that was typical. Every breast exam was the same. *"You have lumpy boobs,"* was usually what the nurses said. I wondered how many other women could relate to the phrase. *Lumpy boobs.* Oddly enough, no man had ever commented on my less than smooth breasts. Maybe they were just being polite. Or maybe they were just men.

"Here. Feel it." She took my fingers and pressed them into a spot on my right breast. "Feel it?"

"Not really." I shook my head. "Don't worry about it, Sandy. It's fine. I'll go get a mammogram. It's been a while anyway. It's no big deal."

In my mind, a mammogram was preventative maintenance, like an oil change, and it was past my due date. Ordinarily, I went like clockwork, but recently my medical check-ups had been switched out for more regular visits with my therapist—leaving a marriage did that. My mental health had trumped my physical health, but it was time to get back on the bandwagon.

Wednesday, October 8, 2008

The interior of the medical arts building was spacious and airy, finished in neutral tones with a hint of a soft blue. Natural maple wood accents made the room feel light and clean. The carpet tiles were a patterned tan color and had a contemporary feel to them. I was even pleasantly surprised to see Nemschoff chairs neatly arranged in the waiting room. How did I know they were Nemschoff? Because I had been selling chairs for fifteen years.

Some people have really meaningful careers—like being teachers or nurses or biochemists. I wasn't one of them. I sold chairs.

Over the years, I had visited many furniture factories. I'd learned about how the wood came out of the kiln in planks and was shaped, sanded, finished, and assembled with a mortise and tendon construction. I'd watched people cut fabric and sew patterns, glue the foam to the springs, and put all the parts and pieces together to construct a four-legged place to sit.

Now, I was happy to see that this facility had purchased quality product and that they weren't cheap. Cheap people bugged me.

After I'd checked in, my eyes scanned the waiting room: four, eight, twelve, twenty-four, fifty-six chairs. At four hundred dollars each, that was twenty-two thousand dollars. With a commission at five percent, that was a total of eleven hundred dollars for the salesperson, not taking into account the end tables and the other accessories... the salesperson had probably made fifteen hundred dollars on the deal. *Not bad. Wish it had been my order,* I thought.

The mammogram was uneventful—other than flattening my boobs to the thinness of pancakes while I made conversation with the woman located behind the lead-filled wall. Tedious. It was just tedious. Before I left the room, the technician added a bonus comment: "Since you're here, let's do an ultrasound. Just to make sure."

All I wanted to do was get back to work. I was not in the mood for another test, but who argues with these people? Within minutes, my chest was all goobed up with Vaseline and a twenty-something-year-old technician with a butterfly tattoo on her neck was pressing a mouse-like device into my right breast.

Garbled images on the TV screen reminded me of pregnant women watching their new babies inside of them.

"Maybe this is something." Her voice sounded less than certain.

My eyes flashed towards the black and white ultrasound.

"But it's kind of vague…. I'm going to have the doctor look at this. Wait here."

Right. As if I was going anywhere at exactly that moment.

These people were starting to get on my nerves. There was NO chance they would buy furniture any time soon, as everything seemed fairly new, so this whole thing felt like a big fat waste of time. They wouldn't find any tumors. I was in the best shape of my life. These tests were just to eliminate possibilities.

The doctor on duty entered the dark room. Butterfly tattoo girl pointed to some area on the screen as the doctor maneuvered the hand-held instrument over my breast. He squinted a bit and eventually responded with: "Nope. I think that's fine."

Ahh..... Another mental sigh of relief. I got dressed and returned to my life full of chairs, tables, coat hooks, and fabric.

Tuesday, October 14, 2008

I was back in Sandy's office waiting for STD results. The lobby needed a design overhaul. The walls were painted a bright baby blue, the white rattan loveseats and chairs were covered in blue floral cushions, and the windows were adorned with plastic green ivy vines. It felt like someone's front porch.

Yes, I was judgmental. I was a furniture snob, and I'd been hanging around designers for a while.

Eventually, a nurse in purple teddy bear scrubs called my name and escorted me to an exam room complete with a big floral wallpaper border, a pink vinyl exam table, and handmade, quilted oven mitts covering the stirrups—complete with red lace trim. I chuckled to myself.

"Please put on the gown with the opening in the front," said the nurse as she closed the door behind her.

Yeah, yeah, I get it. I know the drill. My shirt and bra were hung on the back of the door and I put on the paper pink gown with the opening in the front. Then I reclined on the table and answered emails. Thank God for smartphones.

There was a knock on the door, and Sandy entered my mobile office. She greeted me with a nice smile and told me the wonderful news.

"All the tests came back negative."

I prepared to speed-dial Guy Number Two.

"Awesome. Thanks, Sandy," I replied, ready to launch myself off the table and wave goodbye.

"But before you go, I want to check the lump."

I didn't understand. The mammogram and the ultrasound had both been negative. I rolled my eyes and huffed at Sandy.

"I just want to make sure it's gone. We just want to be thorough." Her fingers moved to the right part of my chest again, and her brows knit across her forehead. Again. "It's still there. It didn't disappear with your cycle."

She took my fingers and tried to show me where the lump was. Again.

I'd never been one of those self-breast-exam people with the pink plastic tag hanging in the shower. Once a year was good enough for me. "I don't feel anything," I muttered.

From the pocket of her lab coat, Sandy pulled out a Sharpie marker and drew a big black X on my chest. She was persistent if nothing else. "It's right there. Can you feel it?"

"You can draw the *Mona Lisa* on my chest if you want to, Sandy, but I still don't feel anything," I huffed.

"Listen," Sandy started to scold me, "you have a family history. There *is* a lump on your chest even if it doesn't show on any exams. You need to get a second opinion - just to weed out any possibilities. It's precautionary." Her kind and gentle face looked stern.

A second opinion? I'd come in for the exam below my waist. All the rest of this was just garbly-goo. "Do I really have to go to another doctor? I don't feel anything."

"Just go," she said, smiling gently. "Do it for your peace of mind."

Peace of mind. I had no idea what that was.

Thoughts of Guy Number Two dissipated. I wasn't so excited anymore.

The receptionist handed me one of those little appointment cards with the surgeon's name and number on it as I left the exam area. Great. Another damn appointment. As I walked to my car, I looked at my phone. *Six missed messages*. I didn't have time for this. There were too many furniture needs to attend to.

Friday, October 17, 2008

Time for my mental health tune-up with my therapist. It had been a year since I'd left my husband. I was full of guilt, shame, and remorse.

At twenty-three years old, I had committed my life to a man who was responsible, financially secure, and ambitious. He'd also been my first boss out of college, twenty-three years older than me, and had been married twice before. His kids were my age and, when we married, I became an instant grandmother. I was probably what some people might call a "trophy wife"—complete with cars, a boat, and a nice house. At twenty-three, I was thrilled that someone else was going to take care of me. It seemed like a brilliant idea at the time.

Until I grew up.

I was, basically, a shitty wife. I had no idea how to be a partner in a relationship. I was self-serving, obnoxious, and inconsiderate. I lied, cheated, and threw my dignity and integrity out the window. *For years*. Seventeen years, to be exact. Eventuallym I became sick and tired of being sick and tired. Enough was enough, and I needed to do something different. In September of 2007, I packed up my clothes and my two cats—Punky and Mazey—and headed off to start fresh.

A year later, I was huddled in the corner of my therapist's sofa wrapped in a soft cream blanket, drama after drama spewing from my lips. "Crack" had disappeared from my life. Guy Number Two was floating around somewhere. My husband wanted me to come home. I was concerned about money. I was living alone for the first time in my entire life. My job was chaotic. I had a cough that wouldn't go away and, oh, by the way, I had all these stupid doctor appointments taking up my time.

"What doctor appointments?" she asked.

My rant had been interrupted. "Oh, yeah. Well, my gynecologist found a lump, and I've had a mammogram and an ultrasound that came back negative, but now she wants me to go to a surgeon for a second opinion."

The floodgates opened unexpectedly. Tears barreled out of me. My life was a mess and I didn't know what to do. I couldn't even breathe.

"Have you told your parents about the health stuff?"

I stopped short and stared at her. "What? Tell my mother? Why? Nothing's wrong. Why would I worry my mother with all these details when there's nothing wrong?"

The last thing I wanted to do was get my mother all worked up.

"You don't need to take care of your mother's reactions. She's your mom. She'll want to know what's going on."

You have GOT to be kidding me. Now I need to have THAT conversation?

Add it to the list. My codependency with my mother smacked me right in the middle of my gut. And to think that I was *paying* for this advice.

I walked out of the office and dialed my mother's phone number.

"Hey, Mom. What's going on?"

"Nothing much, love. What's going on with you?"

"Oh, I'm just leaving my therapist," I said, trying to sound nonchalant.

"That's nice." I think my mother worried about my emotional stability from time to time.

"Yeah. I have to tell you something. My gynecologist found a lump in my breast. I had a mammogram and an ultrasound. They both turned out negative, but they want me to get another opinion, so I go see a surgeon next week. I'm sure it's nothing, but I just wanted you to know."

The silence on the other end of the phone was deafening. Then: "Oh."

"I think it's all okay, Mom. They just want to make sure."

"Well, okay. Thanks for calling. I'll talk to you later."

"Okay, Mom. I love you."

"I love you, too."

And we hung up the phone. My mother didn't want to hear this. Her whole family had been affected by cancer. She had lost so much already.

I hated my therapist.

Tuesday, October 28, 2008

Although Dr. Rob Rimers was a highly recommended surgeon in the area, his lobby did not present him as such. Bland, cream-colored walls were scattered with magazine racks full of *People*, *Better Housekeeping*, and *National Geographic*. Well-worn, navy blue carpet covered the floor and burgundy pleather chairs with fake nail heads around the arms filled the space. The glass wall at the check-in counter had paper announcements taped every which way regarding insurance information and pharmaceutical propaganda. I signed in with the black ballpoint pen that was attached to the counter with a metal chain.

As is typical for salespeople in the furniture industry, I not only judge what spaces look like, but I also try to figure out who makes the chairs and the desks and who the salesperson might have been. It's part of the competitive nature of the business. Typically, there's a label on the bottom of all chairs with all the order information—who the manufacturer was, what the order number was, and, most importantly, who purchased the chair. Curiosity got the best of me as I turned one of the chairs over in the waiting room to review the label. Other patients looked at me strangely as I politely nodded and smiled.

"Bethany?" a middle- aged, stocky nurse yelled my name.

"I just wanted to see who made your chairs," I explained as I followed her into a non-descript exam room and parked myself on the black vinyl guest chair. She pointed out the gown on the table and gave me the directions, "Opening in front."

Again. My Ann Taylor blouse was exchanged for a blue paper gown. The business of selling furniture continued in the room with laminated pictures of the human anatomy hanging on the wall above the latex glove dispenser. Email after email was answered from the exam table. Eventually, Dr. Rimers arrived and introduced himself with a firm handshake. He seemed like a kind, gentle soul, probably in his late thirties.

As he reviewed my file, I brought him up to speed on the undetectable lump. He did the same breast exam, as Sandy had done. He also felt the lump.

"I suggest we schedule a MRI. Just for your peace of mind."

"Really? But I don't feel anything," I whined.

"It's not a big deal. Rule out all the possibilities," he pushed.

Another test. A MRI? There was nothing wrong. The mammogram and ultrasound had both come back negative. I didn't feel anything. These doctors probably just wanted to get rich off my insurance company.

But who says no to a doctor? Especially a surgeon.

Reluctantly, I followed his advice and scheduled the appointment for the MRI.

Later that day, the phone calls from my mother began. "How was your doctor's appointment? Do you have any results? Where do you go next? Do you want us to come stay with you?" (My parents live three hours away, thank God.) I kept trying to reassure her that I was fine and that there was nothing wrong.

"Yes, of course, I will call after my next appointment…. Yes, when I get any results, I'll call you…. No, you don't need to come stay with me."

By the sixth phone call, I was regretting having ever listened to my therapist. I knew my parents were worried, and I knew they wanted to help, but there was nothing wrong. Over and over again, I repeated, "Everything's fine. Nothing's wrong."

But even as the words came out of me, even as I listened to myself saying them out loud, there were moments when my mind wandered and the terrifying question arise. What if it wasn't okay? I had to practice controlling my thoughts and replace this question with something more manageable.

I won't know until I know. I won't know about tomorrow until tomorrow. I will stay in today. I'm going to get through this one day at a time.

Wednesday, November 5, 2008

A week later, I found myself wearing nothing but one of those flimsy gowns and laying horizontal on a cold metal board as I was loaded into a massive tunnel. Big banging noises bounced around my body. I closed my eyes and tried to still my brain. It didn't work. Instead, I made a mental TO DO list covering customers, grocery shopping, chairs, therapy, money, and men. There was nothing peaceful about it. Thirty minutes later, the noises stopped. *Bzzzzz....* The table was removed from the tunnel and I was free to leave.

I couldn't get dressed fast enough. I threw the nurse an obligatory remark—*"It was nice to meet you, hope I don't ever see you again, and have a nice day"*—and smiled and bolted out the door.

As I left the office, I pulled out my Blackberry and checked my email. I needed to drop off a sample chair and deliver fabric samples to a designer down the street. There was a note about a broken table that needed to be addressed and someone wanted a price on a conference table for a project they were working on. *ASAP.* Of course. Life as usual.

Friday, November 7, 2008

While sitting at my desk, Dr. Rimers' number displayed on my caller ID.

"Hey, Dr. Rimers. What's going on?"

He sounded far away. "The MRI looks good for your right breast."

I nearly laughed. I'd known everything was fine. I'd known they were crazy.

I knew it. I knew it. I knew it.

"However," he continued, "we see something in your left breast that looks suspicious."

Suspicious?

That's the word he'd used.

Suspicious.

"Suspicious" was used to describe a character in a murder mystery movie. MRI results weren't suspicious. They were just bad or good.

"We're going to need to do a biopsy," he said with a generic tone, as if he was talking about what TV show he was going to watch that night.

Wait.

My left breast?

That wasn't even the side Sandy had drawn the big X on. It was all wrong. It wasn't right.

A biopsy?

A BIOPSY?

That word always went with cancer. That wasn't good.

I had to tell myself to breath, to remain calm. *It's okay,* I repeated to myself, *it's just one more step towards getting a clean bill of health. It's one more step towards that ever-elusive peace of mind. It's just one more meeting to schedule, like a chair delivery. WAIT. It's a biopsy. It's cancer. WHAT??? WHAT??? Breathe. Breathe. Cancer. Sick. Die. Breathe. Wait. Stop. Breathe.*

Living with these thoughts was NOWHERE near peace and serenity. It was a test of mental maneuvering and survival to get through seconds, minutes, and hours, let alone the next ten days.

TEN DAYS.

Monday, November 17, 2008

The morning of the procedure, my friend Barbara picked me up and we headed to the medical office building's waiting room full of Nemschoff chairs. As we sat in the lobby, I told her how grateful I was that these chairs had a sinuous spring seat construction. I always hated when I had to sit for hours on bad chairs.

Thank God, the doctor had given me a script for Xanax.

The biopsy took place in the same room where the MRI had been done. This time, I laid face down on the table and put my boobs into two cut-out holes.

The technician, Debbie, rubbed my back and gently whispered in my ear, "The doctor is going to stick a needle in your breast to numb it."

Good, numb is good. I wanted as much *numb* as possible.

"He's going into the concerned area of your breast and remove some of the tissue."

Translation: The doctor is going to drill into your breast with something that sounds like a dentist grinding out a cavity and he is going to pull out part of your breast tissue for review.

Xanax. Lidocaine. Numb. Numb. Grind. Grind. Grind.

Surrounded by six technicians and massive, noisy equipment, my brain wandered. "How did this happen? I went to the OB/GYN to make sure I was clean. How did I end up here?" It was then and there that the voice inside my head screamed at me, *"Sex is overrated!"*

Debbie's warm hands touched my back and in a hushed tone she murmured, "It's okay." She told me about her weekend, cleaning the yard, the birthday party for her kid, and the newest book she was reading. She chatted until the drill noise ended, and then she gently helped me off the table.

"You're all done."

I gingerly changed into my clothes and found Barbara in the waiting room. Something big had just happened. This hadn't just been an ordinary doctor's appointment. I was tired. I wanted to take a nap. I didn't want to be doing this. Barbara's fingers wrapped around mine as she pulled me close and we left the building. She walked me to the car and drove me home, where we were greeted by my ever-loving sidekicks, Punky and Mazey. Barbara planted me in bed, surrounded by my black and white balls of fun. We cuddled our way into Never Never Land... where everything was pink and pretty and all was right in the world.

Each morning, I stood in front of the mirror and stared in horror at my breast. The bruising turned from yellow, to green, to black, to blue, and all shades in between. It was tender to the touch, and choosing a day's outfit often led to minor meltdowns. Camisole tank tops under loose sweaters became the most convenient attire. My scars and bruises and pain were all neatly hidden as I headed off to work. Just like everyone else.

Conversations regarding conference tables, custom finishes, and anti-microbial treatments for healthcare cubicle curtains occupied my brain. Sample chairs were moved from one customer to another. Quotes were generated. Work continued. There really was nothing else to do. I was not willing to shut down.

Forty-seven hours after the procedure, I picked up the phone and dialed Dr. Rimers' office.

The cheery voice on the other end answered, "Saratoga Surgical. Can I help you?"

"Hi. This is Bethany Parks. I would like to know if my biopsy results are in." I was short, to the point, and anxious.

"Please hold and I will check for you."

Beethoven's fifth symphony played through the phone.

"Bethany? Sorry, the results aren't in yet. We'll check on them and get back to you."

"Okay. When?" I didn't care if I was being nice.

"By Friday."

I hung up the phone. The silence was deafening.

My focus was redirected back to chairs, conference tables, and coat hooks. A walk in the park. Talk to friends.

Another forty-eight hours passed.

Friday afternoon, I dialed again, and the same cheery voice answered the phone.

"Saratoga Surgical."

My inner bitch was knocking on my door. "This is Bethany Parks. I'm calling for my biopsy results, please. The test was done five days ago."

"Please hold."

Muzac sucks.

"Bethany? Sorry, the results still are not in. We'll check again on Monday."

My internal combustion was starting to spit. "Doctor Rimers said it would only take two days. What's going on?"

"I'm sorry it's taking so long. This isn't ordinary. Next week, for sure. Have a nice weekend."

Yeah, sure. I needed to breathe. *Air in. Air out. It's probably nothing. Perhaps no news is good news. Just another two days.*

My best friend, Marie, was a survivor. She was my sounding board, my sister, my BFF. And she went into production mode now—moving me from place A to place B to place C. She fed me ice cream and took me to the movies and brought me to a pottery class and listened to me bitch. She also made me laugh so hard that I thought I would die. If only that was an option.

Monday, November 24, 2008

I was back in Dr. Rimers' outdated lobby, sitting in the ugly burgundy pleather chair. My best friend Mr. Blackberry and I went on with our bonding experience as furniture emergencies continued to occur in the busy day-to-day work world.

"Bethany?"

As I passed the disheveled desk behind the ugly sliding glass window that had notes taped all over it, I was a bit snarky to the receptionist. "I was hoping to get my biopsy results today," I said with a full-on passive-aggressive tone. "Do you think you could check on it for me?" My inner bitch had become my outer bitch, and I didn't care. She kind of nodded at me.

Alone again in the exam room, I distracted myself with emails.

Dr. Rimers knocked on the door.

"Hello," he said in a way that was impossible for me to read. *Is it good news? Bad?*

He pulled up a chair and sat down across from me. He opened my file as he pulled his stool closer to me.

"I'm sorry to tell you that the results are positive for cancer in your left breast. It's very small, like the diameter of a strand of hair."

My breath caught in my throat.

What? I put my phone down. *What did he just say? Positive?*

He rattled on for a while about the findings, handed me some brochures, and gave me a copy of the biopsy results that appeared to be written in Latin. But I didn't hear any of it.

My emotional switch was already off.

It hadn't hit me.

I shook his hand and looked him squarely in the eye. "Thank you. Thank you for catching it so early. It's so small. I'm really lucky. Thank you."

He had a quizzical look on his face as he walked me to the front desk, where the receptionist scheduled my next slew of appointments. Her desk no longer looked disheveled to me—just busy.

My bitch mode had transitioned into cancer mode.

"Thank you," I said as she handed me the small business cards with dates and times written neatly on them. I walked slowly out of the lobby, my brain no longer preoccupied with chairs or furnishings.

The crisp air hit my skin when I left the building. The late autumn sky was a light grey and the leaves had mostly fallen from the trees. I stood in the parking lot for a minute, my keys in my hand, trying to collect myself.

I had been around cancer before. My family had a history of it. The women who'd come before me had been strong, full of life, and showed me how to do this. My twenty-four-year old cousin, Sarah, had named her implant Pamela. She'd worn beautiful scarves, taken vacations, and sat on the porch of a shack on the coast of Maine and laughed and joked. She'd enjoyed life as it was within the moment. Then we'd gone to her funeral, listened to Rod Stewart sing "Forever Young" during the church service, and watched a four-year-old bury his mother. She hadn't wanted us to cry. She'd wanted us to rejoice in the life that she'd had.

My Aunt Donna, Sarah's mother, won her first battle with breast cancer. She was alive to bury her daughter.

Her second round didn't yield the same results. Her breast cancer spread to her blood and enveloped her body. The end of her life consisted of a bloated belly, a cabinet full of drugs, chemo treatments, and bloody vomit. Cancer won again.

My grandfather, my grandmother, my great aunt, my uncle, my cousin… all had faced this disease and lost. A whole bunch of generations and a whole lot of people were gone. Cancer was nothing new to me.

I unlocked my car and got into the driver's seat. I put my key in the ignition and sat, waiting and thinking.

I guess I really wasn't all that surprised. But my denial had kept me safe, safe from this reality. In the hidden recesses of my mind, I had always wondered *when* I would have cancer, not *if*. Growing up in a family like mine made you think that way.

But the timing was poor. I was trying to get a divorce. I was trying to find a new boyfriend… someone else to take care of me. I was working my semi-high-power sales job and trying to make boatloads of money. I was trying to find my place in life. I didn't have time to deal with this.

Cancer was going to be really inconvenient.

It was the Monday before Thanksgiving, and my life had just changed—more than I realized.

Wednesday, November 26, 2008

Marie and I met in a dark workout room five years ago while sitting on spin bikes and dropping a pound of sweat an hour—or so we hoped. We would grunt and groan and scream at the teacher above the boom of AC/DC, George Thorogood, and Rihanna. Our instructor was training for a triathlon to help raise money for cancer awareness. She was also soliciting wanna-be triathletes and challenging them to raise money to help find a cure. My Aunt Donna had recently died, and I was pissed. I signed up for the event as a way to do something, anything, to relieve the pain. Marie was a recent breast cancer survivor and had lost her mother to this disease. She signed up. The rest was history.

We ran, biked, and swam together. We did Murder Mystery dinners as fund-raisers. We talked about our diets, cancer, and how much weight we would lose. We did 5Ks, 10Ks, sprints, Olympic-distance triathlons, and even a half-marathon together. We rode our bicycles across the state of New York together—in the rain. She helped me empty my closet and pack my car when I left my husband. She told me I would be okay.

Sometimes people show up in our lives exactly when we need them. They are like angels that guide us and show us the way.

Marie was a survivor. She was tough and funny. She had become my cancer coach and agreed to go with me to the oncologist.

We parked ourselves in Dr. Keene's waiting room. I didn't need to flip the chair to see who'd made it. Fifteen years in the industry had given me the very valuable ability to determine quality and price of waiting room furniture in short order. These chairs were mid-market and kind of cheap.

I was already annoyed.

While biding our time in the mediocre quality chairs, I spotted a gentleman across the room. He was about thirty-five years old and was seated next to his soccer-mom-looking wife. He was bald. And not that hot, sexy bald. More like the grey skin, oh-shit bald. He was filling out the stack of paperwork on the clipboard and chatting away as if everything was normal.

How can he be so calm?

After filling out my own pile of forms, Marie and I were ushered down a hallway into an exam room. We passed a big, open room full of metal framed treatment chairs and lots of other bald people hooked up to IVs. The chairs were covered in a tan vinyl with tan metal trim. One of the local hospitals purchased the same chair and they were always breaking. *Cheap.* We made our way to an exam room, which I could only describe as boring.

Whitish walls, a grey laminate built-in counter-top with a sink, an overhead cabinet, an exam table with dull green vinyl coverings, a standard four-leg metal-framed guest chair with dull green fabric, and a stool for the doctor. Yep, definitely boring. There was a piece of random artwork, a shelf with year-old magazines, a stethoscope, and a blood pressure machine all mounted on the walls. Marie's eyes met mine and we both smirked and shook our heads. She took her seat in the guest chair.

Folded on the exam table was the standard issue white medical gown. I began undressing as Marie and I chatted about Crack and Guy Number Two and idiot purchasing agents who wouldn't cut purchase orders. I was no longer modest about being naked in front of people. My boobs were now public property. I slid into the flimsy frock I'd been offered and perched myself on the exam table.

I hadn't talked to Guy Number Two in a few days, not since this had all gotten dumped on me. Starting a new relationship while finding out you have cancer tended to put a damper on the dating thing. Inadvertently, I was opting out of relationships for the time being. Flashing the oncologist would probably be the most excitement I would get for a while.

Dr. Keene entered the room, sat on the stool, and reviewed my file.

"The pathology report from the biopsy says it's a very small tumor," said Dr. Keene while he flipped through my chart. He quoted statistics and stages of cancer.

Marie jotted down notes in a pink journal. My eyes glazed over.

"Due to the size of your cancer and the probability that none of your lymph nodes are involved, surgery should be fairly simple. Dr. Rimers will make a small incision in your breast, go inside, and remove all the cancer cells. During the procedure, we will test your lymph nodes just to make sure nothing has spread. For your peace of mind," he said matter-of-factly.

Okay, peace of mind. I've heard this before.

"You will most likely need to have radiation afterwards as further prevention."

That was fine with me. Whatever needed to be done, I'd do it. I was grateful we had caught it early and that it was a fairly simple process to get through. He did a quick exam on my black and blue boob, and gave me directions in preparation for the upcoming lumpectomy. I shook his hand, said "Thank you," and wished I was anywhere but there.

Marie and I left the exam room and made our way down the long corridor, and then stood in line at the receptionist's counter to schedule some tests needed prior to surgery. Marie was familiar with this office. Dr. Keene was also her oncologist.

"I need to schedule a PET scan, please," I said to Dawn, the office manager sitting behind the sliding glass wall.

"A PET scan? Okay. Next week? Okay."

I nodded as my eyes darted around her desk area. Dawn had flame orange hair, orange glasses, and a really tight dress that left little to the imagination regarding her overflowing cleavage. She resembled a cartoon character. Besides the orange hair, nails, and glasses, her desk was complete with orange flowers, an orange desk pad, and orange picture frames. She even still had up orange decorations from Halloween. Her orange-painted fingernails handed me one of those little appointment cards with orange writing on it to specify the details.

My eyes were about ready to pop out of my head.

"Did she forget to take down the Halloween stuff?" I choked out of my mouth once Marie and I were in the hallway.

"Nope. It's like that all year," Marie giggled.

"Oh shit." I gawked. "All year? She has that shit up there all year?"

Marie nodded and we both burst out laughing. I laughed so hard my stomach hurt.

As Marie and I got to the parking lot, my phone rang. It was my mother.

"How did it go? Where are you? When will you be here?" my mom drilled.

It was the Wednesday before Thanksgiving and I still had a three-hour drive ahead of me to get to my parents' house in Owego, New York. *Shoot me now.* I wished she would just stop already.

"It was no big deal, Mom. We'll talk about it when I get there. I'll be there soon. I love you." I rolled my eyes at Marie as I hung up the phone.

"Thanks so much for coming," I said, hugging my friend. "Thanks so much for making me laugh."

Marie smiled widely and said, "Any time."

We waved good-bye and yelled "Happy Thanksgiving" across the parking lot. I got in my car, turned on the radio, and zoned out for the three-hour ride to my parents' house.

"Hey!" I yelled as I walked in the door.

My mom's typical jovial self was a bit subdued. "Hi, honey. How do you feel?"

I leaned over and kissed her cheek. "Good, Mom. I feel good."

Dad got out of his recliner, gave me an unusually gentle hug, and asked how the ride had been.

"Good, Dad. No rain. Traffic wasn't that bad, either."

I made my way around the room and kissed my sister Julanne, my niece Cheyenne, and my nephew Zach.

"Happy Thanksgiving."

"Happy Thanksgiving" was the standard response. Zach craned his neck to the side so he could continue watching *Law and Order* around me. Julanne started throwing out menu ideas for dinner. Cheyenne smiled sweetly at me from her seat. I made my way into the kitchen and dug through the cabinets for a snack while questions got hurled in my direction from both my parents. I found mint chocolate chip ice cream in the freezer and started scooping away.

"No, I don't have a date for surgery yet…. The office will call next week. Really, it's no big deal…. He says it's a little tumor…. It's just outpatient surgery and I just have to rest for a few days afterwards. Then we can forget about it."

Getting progressively more agitated, the more questions they asked, I wandered back into the living room with my bowl of ice cream and looked for a place to sit. There were never enough seats at my parents' house. My thirteen-year-old nephew had a spot on the sofa.

"Move over, Zack," I said, nudging my way into his space.

He grunted back at me.

"I have cancer. I get a seat."

My mother immediately let out one of those bellowing laughs that come from deep inside her belly. Within a split second, we were back to normal…. One loving, caring, twisted, laughing family. We would get through this together.

Thanksgiving was always pretty low-key. Dinner was a traditional turkey, some Hungry Man instant potatoes, Stove Top stuffing, and a can or two of Del Monte green beans. Mom wasn't feeling so festive this year, so dinner was buffet style. The football game and excess MSG put us all into nap mode in the little living room. It was contentment in action. The evening and the rest of the weekend were spent playing poker, avoiding the topic of cancer, eating leftovers, and practicing denial.

Wednesday, December 17, 2008

The weeks came and went, and my life, for the most part, continued as normal. Well, almost normal. Everything except the word in my brain that kept popping up like Wac-A-Mole. *Cancer. Cancer. Cancer.* I tried to keep everything in perspective, reminding myself every day that the tumor was small. I constantly reminded myself to breathe.

As the day of the lumpectomy neared, my parents made plans to make the three-hour trek to my house, take me to surgery, and stay the night afterwards. Friends were willing to help out, but having my mom and dad around lent an air of safety to the whole experience.

The Same-Day-Surgery department was organized and efficient, like a well-run machine. I checked in, and was escorted into the changing room and placed in a holding tank for everyone having "procedures" that day. I lay in a gurney with nurses coming and going and hooking up IVs and tubes and confirming surgery details and my full name and birth date. Mom sat in the high-back blue vinyl guest chair next to me and tried hard to stay calm. It was obvious she was nervous—she was quiet. She hadn't been to the doctor since my sister had been born… thirty-seven years before. She hated hospitals.

Maybe it was because she'd watched her dad die when she'd been thirty-two. Maybe it was because she'd watched her sister bury her youngest daughter. Maybe it was because her sister had died and her mother had died and her aunt and uncle had all died of cancer. Maybe she'd hoped that the healthcare system would save her family, and instead

31

she'd had to watch as her family dwindled before her eyes. Nevertheless, she was sitting next me now and we were both trying not to laugh when the guy in the cubicle next to me farted.

She gave me a reassuring, gentle smile and squeezed my hand.

"It's okay, Mom. Really, it is," I said.

Eventually, the bellboy or transport guy or whatever you want to call him showed up and said, "Let's get this show on the road."

"I love you, Mom. It's all going to be okay." I felt a tear run down my face.

She bent over to kiss my cheek and whispered, "I love you, too."

I was wheeled away to the staging area outside the operating room. The anesthesiologist assured me I wouldn't feel anything as he prepped me for surgery. The IV was hooked up, drugs were added, and the next thing I knew... I was in recovery. I loved good drugs.

When I opened my eyes, the lights were bright and my dad was standing next to me holding my hand. My mom was at the foot of the bed. I tried to focus my eyes as I looked from my dad to my mom. She looked so far away. Through the haze and grog, I knew something was wrong. Daddy squeezed my hand as he leaned over the railing of my bed and kissed my cheek.

"Honey," he said, his voice unusually somber and low. "The cancer was bigger than they thought. It spread to your lymph nodes. You're gonna' have to do chemo."

I took a deep breath as tears rolled down my cheek and I looked in my father's eyes.

"Daddy, I'm so sad."

"I am, too," he said.

My mom stayed at the foot of the bed, her face pale and her expression unreadable.

There wasn't much more to say. It had been a long day and I was enjoying the effects of whatever narcotics were helping me escape this nightmare. My parents were tired. We all shouted "I love you" at each other as we parted ways—me to recovery, them to whatever surreal experience they were set to experience.

The following day, my parents picked me up and brought me home. We assumed our positions in front of the TV and watched whatever the show of the hour was. Ellen DeGeneres would become the highlight of the day. The cats settled in. I assured my parents that I was secure enough with my physical well-being that they should go home. We didn't know the next steps yet so we had to wait. Doctors wouldn't give us data until they were ready to. It was an opportunity to practice patience and acceptance. For all of us.

Friends came to visit. They helped with the drains and with food and with washing my hair. I tried to get used to my arms being numb from where the nerves had been severed. People distracted me and told me I was okay. And we waited.

Hour by hour, reality changed and morphed, and the spirit of the holidays grabbed me. I needed to participate. Christmas decorations were hung and cookie recipes were strewn about the countertop. Friends went shopping for me and I looked forward to the moment when I could take the next pain pill to take the edge off. I wanted to get lost in the mundane—hoping that if I forgot about cancer, it might go away.

I clung tight to the delusional world in which I lived. Everything looked the same from the outside. It was just my insides that were a mess.

Monday, December 22, 2008

Marie and I sat in the oncologist's waiting room, making snide remarks under our breath about orange decorations until my name was called and we were escorted to the boring exam room again. Marie took her seat on the icky guest chair and I made my way to the exam table/perch. Doctor Keene knocked on the door and entered the room. He sat on the mini stool and looked at me over his half-glasses with the folder in his lap.

"Dr. Rimers removed three sentinel nodes. They were tested during surgery and one of them came back positive. At that point, he removed fourteen more nodes for testing purposes. All of these came back negative for any signs of cancer. The tumor he removed from your left breast was between one centimeter and two centimeters… larger than was expected," he said.

He handed me a copy of the pathology report, which was three pages long and included words that were most likely not in a typical dictionary. I handed it to Marie.

"Incisions need to heal for four to five weeks. Then you'll have eight chemo treatments, one every other week."

I did a quick mental calculation in my head: eight treatments, one every other week… sixteen weeks, divided by four. *Four months.*

FOUR MONTHS? WHAT? Followed by six weeks of radiation treatment five days a week. Another month and a half. *Five and a half months.*

My shock absorber—denial, self-protector, whatever you wanted to call it—was on high alert. I shot Marie a perplexed look. She nodded as if to say, *"Yup. This is what people do. It happens all the time."*

Dr. Keene threw around phrases like "hormone receptive" and "HER2neu positive/negative."

I wanted to shout at him, "Please, let me go back to my other vocabulary... when I talked about scissor mechanisms on treatment chairs or fabrics and double rubs, and Nanotex topical coatings. Please let me talk about sled base versus four leg chairs, and metal frame versus wood frame. I am just tired of hearing it all! Please just SHUT THE FUCK UP!"

That's what I wanted to say, but instead I simply nodded along with him and pretended to appear interested in what he was saying to me. Inside, I felt like I was falling, crashing, and there would be no getting up from it.

We finished our meeting, checked in with the orange receptionist to schedule the next appointment, and left the building with a better understanding of what the rest of treatment would look like.

Marie hugged me and promised, "You'll be fine."

I nodded. Numb.

Later that evening, as I sat on the sofa with my cats, information began to slowly seep into my body. Piece by piece, the puzzle was falling into place and I was learning acceptance. I had cancer. Or, I used to have cancer. If I was lucky, they'd just cut it all out of me. Was I supposed to use the present or the past tense when talking about this? Doctors were telling me to do more treatment—for my peace of mind. God, I hoped this was all worth it. How would I actually ever judge that metric of peaceful?

As time passed, I continued to move along the path of least resistance: desks, chairs, tables, waste receptacles, coat hooks, and textiles. I worked on quotes, and responded to questions and phone calls. I started to tell customers about my health issues. I needed to let people know because I was slowing down. My priorities were shifting. I needed to make my health my first concern, but I still wanted to sell some chairs... actually, I *had* to sell some chairs.

I was single. I was a commission-only salesperson, and I had a few bills to pay. I had to stay in touch with people. I had no intention of being quiet through this process. I would not hide or be a victim. I would carry on to the best of my ability. Stubbornly.

Wednesday, December 24, 2008

The social part of cancer was challenging. Everyone had their own reactions to this word, and therefore to me. Some people were scared. Some wanted to help. Some didn't know what to say. For many who had not been around cancer before, I knew that my presence made them uncomfortable. But, the truth was, I was okay. With each moment, I was okay, and that was important. I wasn't going to worry about later or the next day. I was going to take it slow, and take each day as it came.

I AM okay.

I AM okay.

I AM okay.

That became my mantra.

Most Christmases were spent at my parents' house, but this year everyone had agreed to come to me so I wouldn't have to travel.

"What should we have for dinner?" Mom asked during one of our daily phone conversations.

"I don't care, Mom. Whatever you want is fine with me. Really. We could have cold cuts or pizza. It doesn't matter. I just want everyone to be together."

It was the truth. Food was the last thing on my list of things to be concerned about. I just wanted simple.

It was Christmas Eve and my house was full of family and friends. The three-piece, snap-together pre-lit tree filled the front window and a fire in the fireplace warmed the living room. My parents and Julanne and Zach and Cheyenne were there. Marie popped in. Friends from work randomly stopped in. Shrimp cocktail, Rummy 500, and twisted humor followed by insane belly laughs filled the air. Under the tree were five packages—a pair of socks for Dad, a deck of cards for Mom, and three gift cards for my sister and niece and nephew. Never had I done so little in preparation for such a big holiday. And yet, the spirit of the season filled the house. It wasn't about the stuff anymore.

Thursday, January 1, 2009

I didn't want to say Happy New Year because I wasn't happy, and I didn't give a shit if anyone else was happy, either. I wanted to take hostages, to drink, to run, and maybe to drive my car into a tree. I wanted to be mean, vicious, and self-centered. I wanted the world to revolve around me. I wanted to get laid and then get rid of the person after. I wanted to be alone, to be miserable.

I didn't want this cancer. I didn't want any part of it. I didn't know how to deal with it and I felt as though I was going round and round in my head trying to figure it out, to understand it. But I couldn't.

I wanted to shout at someone, "Why me?" I wanted to feel bad for myself. I was sad, scared, and pissed. I wanted someone to take care of me.

Friday, January 2, 2009

Normally, New Year's Day was a day of planning for me: what half marathon was I going to do, what triathlon would I sign up for, what trips would I go on, and where was life going this year? I would spread out big pieces of paper on the floor, along with stacks of magazines, a pair of scissors, and glue. I'd flip through the magazines and start tearing out pictures and text. I was full of dreams, hopes, and desires. Year after year, I created visual bucket lists for myself and set goals.

This year was different, though. This year, a war wall was installed instead. Every good conference room had one. Mine just happened to be in the hallway that led from my dining room to my bedroom. At the top of the wall, two index cards shouted the highest goals: *Peace* and *Serenity*. Monthly calendars for January, February, and March were hung in line on the wall. Doctor appointments filled small squares. Pictures of friends, lists of phone numbers, and motivational sayings all found their way to the wall. Yellow smiley faces were splattered throughout. I snipped and clipped and created. After a few hours, I stepped back, put my hands on my hips, and examined my work. It wasn't the vision board that I had planned on, but it was creative nonetheless.

I felt good.

Later that afternoon, while sitting in the Price Chopper parking lot, I called Dr. Rimers' office to refill my antibiotic. I was surprised when the nurse put me on hold and the actual doctor picked up the phone.

"Hey, Bethany. How do you feel?"

"I feel pretty good today. Just need to fill my script for pain meds." There was no way that I was going to sit through pain if I didn't have to.

"That's great. I'm glad you called. I was going to call you later anyway. I wanted to let you know that your case has been different than most."

This statement did not make me feel warm and fuzzy. I watched a woman push her cart through the parking lot. There was a screaming kid in the front of it and Mom looked pretty frazzled.

"The fact that nothing showed up on your mammogram or your ultrasound, and that the MRI showed a very small set of abnormal tissue, were not very distinct signs as to the extent of your cancer."

I watched the snow fall outside as my windshield wipers clip-clopped back and forth across my windshield.

"Pathology can't tell us if we have clear margins. I would suggest that we discuss the possibility of doing another surgery. Just to be safe."

I leaned forward and pressed my forehead against the steering wheel, trying to calm my breathing. I didn't get it. *No clear margins? Another lumpectomy? Why not a mastectomy? What was going on?*

"Can you please explain what that means? No clear margins?"

"When we did the lumpectomy, we took small pieces of breast tissue and then analyzed them after surgery. We are not certain we got all the cancer cells."

Stunned. I was stunned.

The snow kept falling outside. Big, fat, wet flakes.

"So, let me make sure that I have this clear. Let's say that you took three pieces of breast tissue out. You then tried to put them back together in the same configuration as when they were inside me. Then you looked at the edges... and you aren't certain that you got everything. Am I getting this right?"

Time was standing still.

"Yes, that's correct." His voice was a little shaky. "If you were my wife, I would have a difficult time having this conversation with you."

There was not one second of hesitation. From somewhere deep in my toes came the words, "No worries, Dr. Rob. I'm going to get a second opinion."

"That's a good idea," he replied, sounding almost relieved.

I quickly ended the conversation and took one slow, deep breath. Okay, maybe I took a few deep breaths and got lost in the snowflakes. Eventually, I made my way into the grocery store, grabbed a shopping cart, and filled it with fresh baked bread, fresh garlic, tomato paste, crushed tomatoes, parmesan cheese, and chicken cutlets. Homemade sauce was in order. And, oh yeah, the drugs at the pharma counter.

Life continues... right?

Friday, January 9, 2009

My brain is a problem. I think too much. Each day is the same Groundhog's Day of wonder. Not having answers. Not knowing. Not being able to ask anyone. Surrender to ideas of change. Not believing any of this is real. Cooking meals. Cleaning the kitty litter. Paying bills. Talking about chairs. Watching Ellen at 4:00. Round and round and round.

Sunday, January 11, 2009

My cousin Shannon's invitation to join her and her boyfriend Matt on vacation in the Caribbean was a shot in the arm. There was no reason to stay in New York, stuck in the snow and battling my emotions when a sunlit beach was calling my name. In the blink of an eye, my flight was booked and my smaller than small duffel bag was packed.

Six days later, the eighty-two-degree air welcomed me to St. Thomas as if it were a warm hug. I stepped into the airport bathroom, changed out of my snow garb, threw on a sundress, and hailed a cab to the ferry that would eventually take me to my final destination—Cruz Bay, St. John. I boarded the ferry and found a seat in the front of the open-air vessel. Ziggy Marley played on my I-pod and my head bobbed aimlessly as my soul let out a sigh of relief. Song after song released the tension from my body as the sun kissed my skin. For an hour, I sat on that ferry—utterly and completely content, free from worry, free from snow, and free from ickiness.

Shannon and Matty-O were waiting at the dock in shorts, T-shirts, smiles, and glowing tans, and with freshly squeezed lemonade. "OH, I'm so glad you came!" my blonde-haired, blue-eyed cousin crooned as she wrapped her arms around me.

"Me, too. Me, too. Thanks so much for inviting me. I'm so happy to see you."

Matty took my bag, put his arm around my shoulders, and pulled me close. They had been through cancer too many times, but the Caribbean had become their vacation haven. This was where they came when they needed a get-away. And they were sharing it with me.

"I can't believe I'm really here. Who does this? Who just picks up and leaves their job on a moment's notice? Oh My God. It's AWESOME!" I hooped and hollered and squealed in excitement.

Pink and blue and green buildings filled my eyes. Calypso music played in the distance. The smell of salty ocean and barbeque filled the air. The narrow streets of Cruz Bay led to a parking lot jammed with ancient, beaten vehicles. Nothing new here. Everything was low key, laid back, island gear. Matty threw the bags in the back of a tattered jeep and my first ride through the hills of St. John was in full swing. Rough, narrow, treacherous roads took us up and over craggy, jungle-like mountains that eventually led to their cabin, or better yet, a pretty cool version of an open-air treehouse built into the side of a hill. The porch hung out over what seemed like a tropical rainforest and the ocean heaved and sighed in the distance, the sounds of waves crashing on a shoreline. Shannon and I stepped out onto the porch, plopped down into comfy chairs, and admired the natural beauty surrounding us. Matty appeared with a platter of cheese and crackers and fresh iced tea. It was like our old family vacations—a beach, lots of food, and tons of laughter. Our conversations drifted between cancer, death and dying, the Caribbean, where was the best restaurant to go to, and which beach we should go to in the morning. It was fresh air, family, and that feeling of familiarity and contentment. Sleep was easy and comfortable and offered a dreamlike state, far away from snow and ice and doctors.

By ten o'clock the next morning, we were parked at Maho Bay. The beach was a quarter mile long with chickens marching up and down the white sand. A total of eight people dotted the landscape. White triangles of sails danced in the distance upon the sparkling water.

"Oh my God. I think this is heaven on earth," I squeaked. "How did I get so lucky to be here?"

Shannon laughed. "We're talking about moving here."

"Oh, you should! You should! Why not? It's awesome here."

"But what about work and a job and health insurance? There's all those responsible things that I should be doing." Shannon sighed.

My cousin had buried her sister, her brother-in-law, and her mother. She had seen cancer and tragedy up close. I wanted her to be happy. I crossed my fingers, hoping that maybe, just maybe, she would choose to take a break from life and relocate to this tropical place, which I would kindly refer to as *Heaven on Earth*.

Matty leaned over from his beach chair. "Wanna' snorkel?"

My body tensed. *That's a crazy request*, I thought. *What about the incision from my lumpectomy? And my numbness? And my cancer?*

"I don't think I can. I'll just watch," I muttered.

"It's just a little scar," Shannon smirked, offering me a comforting smile.

She was right. What was I thinking? I could go snorkeling; I could get in the water. I didn't need the doctor's permission. It was *just swimming*.

Matty grabbed the gear, tossing me all the necessary pieces. The grains of sand kissed my toes and, as we waded into the tepid water, I submerged my body in the waves, letting them rise and fall and carry me. I'm not the most coordinated or graceful person on the face of the planet, so getting those goofy fins on my feet without drowning was no easy task. The waves crashed over me and salty water filled my nose and mouth. I gasped for air as laughter shot from my gut. Over and over again, I tried to get the plastic gear in place. Finally, the fins, the goggles, and the snorkel were all situated. I was a kid again, awkward and clumsy and un-tethered from life.

My body was buoyant as we made our way to the rough and ragged reef. Packs of black and white zebra fish floated past as the sound of my breathing echoed in and out of my head. Little orange-striped fish hid in patches of green, jelly-like tentacles growing up from the ground. Schools of brilliant yellow three-inch swimmers with long, thin, pointy noses passed by, followed by thousands of tiny silvery creatures that reflected the sun as if they were a collective mirror. Pink coral waved from the floor. My breath went in and out. In and out. The sounds of the sea were deep and visceral. I had escaped my body and my mind. My reality was this beautiful, oceanic world. My arms and legs propelled me forward. The warm water cleansed my soul. Breathing in. Breathing out. Color. Warmth. Peace. Escape.

It didn't last long enough.

"I did it!" I yelped with glee as I collapsed on a beach towel next to Shannon. "I was out there. I didn't feel sick. I forgot about the cancer. I didn't think about it. Oh, Matty, you don't know how much this means to me. Thank you. Really, thank you."

"Of course, you did it. There's no way you could have come here and not gone snorkeling. We wouldn't have let it happen." Matty believed in me more than I did. Shannon nodded her head in agreement.

We napped and rested and listened to the waves slap along the sand and the chickens clucking along the beach until the sun started to sink toward the horizon, offering the signal to head home for the day.

Matty had been a restaurant owner in a past life, complete with all the chef experience any one person could have. A lavishly prepared meal of rice, fish, and fresh vegetables graced the porch table of the treehouse as the air started to cool. The heat, the sun, and the exercise had sapped the energy from my less-than-perfect body. Bite by bite, I felt rejuvenated and reinvigorated, but still in need of slumber. Luckily, everyone was on the same page, and our middle-aged bodies were tucked in and asleep before ten o'clock, the fresh air gently kissing us good-night.

While we were experimenting with semi-outdoor living, the sun became nature's alarm clock. Coffee, eggs, toast, and a leisurely entrance into the day while watching the ocean move and the leaves wave from a treehouse had never been on my *List of Things to Do*. It should have been.

Our porch vista included Ram's Head—a mountain peninsula peeking into the ocean. It was a typical tourist hike, and we were game. Backpacks, water bottles, and hiking shoes were the attire of the day. We trekked down the ravine, along rocky beaches, through fields of short flowering cactus, and eventually arrived at the tip of the trail. Sweat dripped from my brow as views of St. Thomas and Tortola engulfed opposing horizons. The wind whipped around us and waves crashed on the cliffs below, creating spinning whirlpools of majestic blue and teal and foamy white.

I sat in silence pondering the meaning of life. At that moment, I was grateful to have been diagnosed with cancer. Before that fateful day, I would have been too busy to make the trip. I would have had a ton of excuses, most of them about money: bad economy, tough times, just after the holidays, whatever. Instead, I was spending two whole days in the islands surrounded by peace, serenity, and family who understood what I was going through.

For two days, I felt surrounded by love and the healing powers of Mother Nature.

Thursday, January 15, 2009

My escape came crashing to an abrupt end with a return to ice, snow, cats, friends, and reality. Upcoming appointments included a PET scan, a second opinion regarding surgery, and another meeting with an oncologist.

I talked to customers and friends about work. *"How's the project at the hospital progressing?" "Do you need any samples?" "Want to see some new fabrics?" "What about that conference room at the university?" "Sure, we can send out wood finishes for you to review."*

Oh yeah, I still worked. What else was there to do?

And then one day, as I was driving along the thruway headed to deliver a sample chair, it came—a text message from Crack. It had been months.

My heart stopped.

"I hope you have a stellar year."

WTF?

"I have breast cancer," I immediately typed back. I guess I was pissed and wasn't going to pretend and be pleasant or nice.

My phone rang within seconds. *INSANITY* appeared in the caller ID display. I answered anyway.

"Hello?" I shook inside.

"Hi. I got your text." His voice sent chills through my body.

"Yeah. I got yours, too." *Be cool. Be cold. Don't let him in,* my brain screamed at me.

"How are you?"

Was he asking because he cared? Had he really been thinking about me? Why did he even bother? I didn't need anyone's sympathy.

"I'm good. I'll be fine."

"I want to see you. Can I come visit?"

Don't do it. Don't do it. Don't do it.

"Sure. When's good for you?" And with that brief conversation, Crack was back in my life—if that's what you wanted to call it.

Sunday, January 18, 2009

Afterburn. That's the word I use. It's that slow response to things, like when shit creeps up on you from days earlier. Like a delayed hangover.

On Friday, I went to see Dr. Sharron Kauffman, my second opinion surgeon. She had worked as a trauma surgeon in Bosnia for the Army, which in my mind meant she was tough. No bullshit. I liked that. Her reception area was long and narrow and decorated in hues of brown and tan. It felt masculine and strong.

I followed her through the receptionist area into her office. She offered me a guest chair in front of her cherry laminate desk as she made her way to a slim, black leather chair behind the desk. Her work area was neat and clean, and there were no signs of orange flowerpots or orange paper clips anywhere.

"Nice furniture," I commented. "You bought it from Bob Jones?"

She looked at me, a little perplexed. I probably sounded like a stalker who was overly obsessed with her chairs, which was actually the sad truth.

"I sell furniture for a living. I checked out the chairs in the lobby. It's part of what I do."

She smiled and we discussed the purchasing process for her office furniture. I'd been right. Bob had brought three or four samples up for her to review before the order was entered. Ugh. Schlepping chairs.

Dr. Kauffman opened my file, flipped through the pages for a minute, and then looked directly at me.

"Well, this is terrible, isn't it?"

"I hadn't quite gotten to *terrible*," I responded.

"Well, nothing showed up on the exams. The MRI showed only a small set of affected cells. Then, BANG! Bigger than it was supposed to be. It's alarming."

Shit. I was still in the "Life is Good" mode and trying to trudge the road to happy destiny.

"Well, okay," I said half-heartedly. "After the lumpectomy, Dr. Rimers said they didn't have clear margins. He wanted to do another lumpectomy to take more tissue. It might sound crazy, but I'm thinking about having a double mastectomy. I don't want to worry about it coming back. I don't want to have to go through more surgeries than necessary. I want to have as much peace and serenity in my life as possible when this is over. What do you think?" I looked this woman in the eyes. She didn't flinch.

"If it were me, I would have had a double mastectomy two weeks ago."

I smiled, loving Dr. Kauffman.

"Great. Let's just schedule it. I want this done. I'm so glad that I came to see you. I wanted to get a woman's perspective on this."

"I have a lot of women that come to see me who believe that, because I am female, I will want to save their breast tissue." She shook her head as if she was annoyed by this attitude. "I need to break them out of their denial. My job is not to save breast tissue or to make them look good. My job is to remove cancer, all of it. The plastic surgeon does the rest of it."

Her response surprised me, but she had made her role very clear. *Have cancer?* She'd remove it. Aesthetics, vanity, and boob jobs came from someone else.

She escorted me to the receptionist, shook my hand, and let me know they would call with the date for surgery. We also scheduled an appointment with the plastic surgeon.

Later that afternoon, I barged into the hair salon with energy seeping from every poor in my body. Most of the clients were pristine, prim, old-money Saratoga types, rattling on about the latest and greatest restaurant or their new Land Rover. There were lots of diamonds and neatly coiffed hair-dos and yoga bodies lined up on the chairs.

"How's things?" Shari asked as I plunked myself down in front of the mirror.

"I have cancer. Breast cancer," I said bluntly. "I'm going to have to do chemo and will lose my hair. I want to go red. Beautiful, gorgeous red. Okay?"

Wide-eyed, Shari stared at me, stunned. A slight hush came over the room.

"Red… like auburn," I continued. "I think I can pull it off. Don't you?"

"Oh, I'm so sorry," Shari finally muttered. "Are you okay?"

"Yes, I am. I just think that I need red hair. Where's that swatch thing? This is going to be fun."

Shari reached into her cabinet and pulled out the fan deck of colors and suggested Celtic Copper.

"Yes!" I exclaimed. "That's it. It's magnificent."

She left me in my seat and I pulled out my Blackberry to escape into my digital email world.

Within hours, my blonde head of hair was transformed into a halo of richness. I stared at myself in the mirror and fell in love with the person before me. My blue eyes seemed to bounce, and my white skin had never looked so clean before. The ginger strands screamed, "I am strong! I am sexy! I will live my life! I will not go down without a fight!" Who knew that hair could say so much?

Monday, January 19, 2009

PET Scan day. Someone injected radioactive dye into my body, let me percolate, and then put me in one of those tubes again. Who ever knew that this PET scan thing was actually radioactive sugar that was used to activate cancer cells? Geez. The stuff I learned going through this process was amazing. Yet, patience was by far the biggest lesson of all.

Tuesday, January 20, 2009

The waiting periods were dreadful. I had made that transition from being a furniture vendor to the healthcare industry to being on the inside of this machine. I tried to wait patiently for my next appointment, but I got angry, scared, and pissed. I tried to wait patiently for my life to get back to "normal," but it wasn't happening like I wanted it to. I tried to wait patiently for peace and serenity, but those things were nowhere to be found.

Move a muscle, change a thought. It rang true. I needed to get out of myself.

As a healthcare customer, I decided to go shopping—shopping for a good place to get chemo. I was willing to forgo Marie's recommendation in order to have some of the amenities on my list. I wanted a little coffee shop for my friends and parents to use. I wanted something that felt like a spa. I wanted nice furniture. It bugged me to no end that my current oncologist, Dr. Keene, had cheap chairs. I didn't even have to flip them to see the tag; I just knew. Cheap. I also hated orange decorations. I would pull my hair out if I had to look at that every week. *Oh wait, I'm not going to have hair.*

I made an appointment to visit another oncologist's office to check out their facilities. I wanted more of the upscale healthcare amenities. If I was going to do cancer, I wanted to do it in style.

A phone call with one of the Nurse Practitioners assured me that the PET scan had turned out fine. There was no other cancer in my body.

I'm not so sure I believed them.

The next stop was with the plastic surgeon, and the topic was how to make me some new boobs. As I opened the door to the office, I was pleasantly surprised to find that Dr. Murphy's waiting room had Thonet chairs in it. Undoubtedly, there'd been an actual, certified interior designer involved with planning this space. It had a nice flow, a soothing atmosphere, and creative blue fabric against the maple frames. All this filled me with a sense of comfort as I checked in at the front desk and made my way to a comfy chair.

I had barely begun thumbing through the most recent version of *People* magazine when my name was called out. The nurse of the day ushered me to yet another unexceptional exam room, handed me a gown, dispersed the standard directions, and closed the door behind her. Within minutes, a slight woman with short, stylish gray/white hair and wire rim glasses opened the door after a quick knock.

She held out her hand. "Hi, Bethany. I'm Dr. Murphy."

Her shake was firm and polite, just like her smile. Her face was clean and fresh without a trace of makeup and her bright blue eyes made me feel at ease immediately.

"Hi, Dr. Murphy." My fear evaporated in the presence of this woman. A pink ribbon lapel pin on her lab coat caught my attention as I rattled on about where I was in the process.

"Okay. Well, we should probably talk about your reconstruction options, yes? There are three options."

"Yes, please." I wanted to know about my new boobs and was hoping that they would be a tad perkier than my current version, which were thirty-six longs.

"Option one: Don't do it. Some women opt out of reconstruction and use prosthetic breasts."

"Nope." I shook my head. "That's not going to work for me." I was newly single, and having boobs would probably be a somewhat important part of the dating circuit at some point in the future.

"Option two: Do the surgery now and wait for things to recover, and then do reconstruction at a later date."

"Why would someone do that?" I asked.

"Some people don't want to deal with everything at once. They just want to get rid of the cancer and then make plans for reconstruction when that's done."

"Ick." I shook my head and scrunched my nose up in disgust. "What else?"

"The third option is to start the reconstruction at the same time as your double mastectomy. After Dr. Kauffman has removed all the breast tissue, I would lift your pectoral muscles and insert flat plastic envelopes, called expanders, underneath the muscles. The expanders have little metal valves on them, and over time we will inject saline into them and expand your chest to create two pockets that will eventually accept implants."

Ouch. Metal valves? Injections? Lifting up muscles? I'd been hoping more for a quick-fix new boob job, not all these technical details.

I needed to put this conversation into some context I could understand.

"Dr. Murphy, I sell desks and chairs and tables for a living. When I go see customers, I usually talk about shapes and sizes of desks. I usually have little swatches of wood finishes or fabric choices. I was hoping that there was a shelf in your office, some place that had all the samples of the implants. Am I off-base here?"

Dr. Murphy chuckled. "Nope, we don't do it that way. Do you remember the Crissy doll as a kid? The one that was just a head? There was a dial on the back of her torso, and you could turn the dial and her hair would grow. Remember?"

I nodded.

"Well, I like to think of reconstruction in that manner. I refer to it as Dial-a-Boob. Each week, we will make them bigger and bigger. When you eventually get to the size you want, we stop there and schedule surgery to remove the expanders and install the actual implants."

"Kind of like test driving a new set of boobs?" I asked. Her head bobbed up and down.

Okay, I understand. Decision made. Dial-a-Boob it is.

At the end of the day, I opened my emails. "Donald W. Moss – USAF" appeared in the inbox. *MY BROTHER!!!!!! SPIKE!!!!!! From Afghanistan!* It was a short note to just check in and see how things were going. He made a slight reference to some of the young, struggling soldiers that were part of his unit. I imagined what the troops went through over there, what the sounds were like and what their days were like. Young kids doing what they were trained to do, but witnessing violence, death, and massacres up close.

I took a deep breath and looked out my window at the backyard covered in snow. We had so much to be grateful for. Sure, things could always be better, but I didn't hear the sounds of bombs going off at night, or worry about getting blown up while driving my car or wonder if the kid in the bunk next to me would be alive the next day or not. Keeping things in perspective was important.

Wednesday, January 21, 2009

Crack was here last night.

Sex. Sex. Sex. Thank GOD!!!!!!

Intensity. Sweat. Tingles. Toes curling. Panting. Screaming. Skin on skin. Feeling my body. In the moment. Fully present. Then…. Over.

A nagging feeling had slithered into my exhausted brain. Something wasn't right. It felt like an eight-hundred-pound elephant sitting on my chest. It was an opening into breaking my denial.

"Are you seeing someone else?" I asked as I snuggled myself into his armpit. I would never have asked the question before because sometimes the truth hurts—and I preferred to pretend everything was as I wanted it to be.

There was a brief pause, and he replied, "Yeah… I am."

I wasn't angry. I wasn't even upset. I was just glad I knew the truth.

"So, what are you doing here?" I asked.

He had no answer.

I didn't press the matter further, deciding I really didn't need to know his reasons. That wasn't the point; that wasn't why I had said he could visit.

Some people have going away parties for their hair before chemo starts, but that wasn't really my thing. I wanted to pay tribute to my sexuality. I was angry and mad and sad that I would be losing my nipples during surgery. The decision to have this part of my body removed had been made, though, and I would need to accept everything that went with that.

Sex had always been part of my life, ever since I'd been fourteen. I loved men. I loved attention. I loved to feel attractive. I loved having all of my senses on fire, simultaneously. That had always been what I'd chased. In the back of my mind, I thought about all the other "stuff" that was "supposed" to be part of the perfect relationship: the ability to communicate, some emotional stability, mutual respect, and a healthy interdependency. I knew those things existed, but personally, I'd never really had the whole package. Maybe it was just a "knight in shining armor" fantasy. Maybe there was no such thing as a perfect relationship.

Or maybe I just needed to spend more time in therapy. Damn it.

Surgery was only three weeks away, and Crack had come back into my life just in the nick of time. Our bodies moved together as he rolled to his side and wrapped his arms around me. I felt safe and secure and warm.

"I want to have a going away party for my nipples," I said. "I want to have one more over-the-top romp. I want to enjoy my sexuality for a few more hours in a big way. If I book us a room at Mohonk House, will you spend the night there with me?" I held my breath, hoping he would say yes.

"Sure," he whispered into my ear as he squeezed me close. I let out a sigh. My body sank deeper into his and a deep sleep washed over me.

At five o'clock in the morning, I rolled over to an empty bed.

And I scheduled an appointment with my therapist for the next day.

Sunday, January 25, 2009

The first time I met Aimee, she was dressed in a long-sleeve black Harley T-shirt, carrying a big-ass black Harley coffee mug, and had her long, auburn red hair tied back in a black leather wrap. She had mischievous green eyes and a laugh that warmed my heart.

I introduced myself with something close to, "Will you be my friend? And can you teach me to ride my bike?"

Aimee did her Aimee-kind-of-thing—she smiled her brilliant smile, and said, "Sure."

The purchase of my Harley Davidson Softail Deluxe was probably the beginning of my mid-life revival. It was daring. It was sexy. It was a seven-hundred-pound statement of my freedom, gorgeous with all its chrome, white wall tires, and braided leatherwork. My Harley. A total impulse purchase. I wanted to be cool and I thought that, if only I had a Harley... well, then I would be in the "IN" crowd. I didn't know where that crowd was, but it was obvious that Aimee was part of it.

She knew where the oil pan was and how to change the fluids in her bike. She spent hours with her special tools washing her beloved Indigo Blue freedom ride. "A labor of love," she would call it. She knew about her engine and the power commander and Vance & Hines exhaust systems. The only thing I knew about mine was that it was black and white and chrome.

Amazingly, Aimee was put in my life at about the same time I left my seventeen-year marriage. Learning how to ride became a form of therapy. It focused my brain. It gave me something to talk about other than *my feelings*. For about a year, my new red headed friend taught me "the language." She taught me how to ride. She taught me about where to get the non-pumpkin-head helmet and the stickers and the leather chaps. She taught me how to park my two-wheel symbol of coolness so that I wouldn't drop it in front of crowds of people at the ice cream stand—a regular occurrence. We spent time on the roads. We practiced. We sat propped on walls of gas stations eating M&Ms and drinking coffee. We talked about life and became friends.

At the end of that first year, life shifted for both of us. Aimee's marriage was shaky and I was diagnosed with breast cancer. She needed a place to stay, and I needed someone to stay with me. She had taken nursing classes years before and was okay with the fact that I had cancer. She made me laugh and she loved my cats and she came to live with me.

Sunday, February 1, 2009

Time was ticking away and life was changing. My double mastectomy was scheduled for Wednesday, February 18. Pre-op stuff started on Tuesday, Feb 17. Two weeks away. Actually, it was seventeen days at this point. Actually, it was four hundred and eight hours... or thereabouts.

On Tuesday morning, I opened a care package that had arrived the day before. It was from a woman I had met only a handful of times in my life. She was a friend of my cousin's in New Hampshire and had become very active in the Making Strides Breast Cancer walk in that area. She donated a ton of time and effort to helping raise money for cancer research, and she'd sent me a care package with some scarves, a book for caregivers, some bath products, and a lovely letter telling me that the furniture at her OB/GYN office deserved a thumbs-down. It cracked me up. And then I cried. It was beyond anything I could ever have imagined. How could an almost stranger take the time to put together such a thoughtful package? Who knew there were people so kind and compassionate and generous? It was shocking to be on the receiving end of this.

Thursday, February 5, 2009

Today was "Tour a different oncology suite day". Based on the last oncologist's waiting room furniture and the orange receptionist, I had made an appointment to check out another provider. I was ecstatic to see a cohesive design pallet and quality seating in the waiting room of a local hospital. The receptionist called my name and I was escorted into a nicely appointed exam room. Nothing extravagant, but nice.

Oncology Doctor Number Two came in and introduced himself as Dr. Miller. I wasn't really that interested in getting to know him. I'd just wanted a tour of the space.

"It's nice to meet you, Doctor Miller. I want to let you know that I'm really just here to take a look around and see what your oncology suite is like. I'm pretty sure the chemo you're going to give me here is the same chemo they would have given me at another doctor's office. I want to see if you have an area where my family and friends can rest comfortably while they're here. Is there a place for them to eat? Is there an outdoor area?"

I think Dr. Miller was a little flabbergasted. I needed to explain.

"I sell furniture and work with architects and designers for a living. Sometimes I sell hospital furniture, and it's important to me that the facility has considered all these options and that it's convenient and well thought out, and a pleasant and calming environment."

He nodded… and continued to pull out his manila folder and tell me about cancer cells and Adriamycian,

Cyterabine, and Taxol. I didn't really give a shit. It was going to suck and I just wanted to listen to a waterfall and have some nice scenery to look out the window at.

After the tour, I agreed to do chemo at this hospital, and I signed all the paperwork, waivers, and approvals.

It was a long day.

Friday, February 6, 2009

The week prior to surgery was full of practical activities—organizing taxes, updating my will, and getting a health care proxy. Questions like "Do you want to be resuscitated" and "Who will be the beneficiary of your earthly goods?" were asked. *What earthly goods?* There wasn't a whole bunch of anything to leave to anyone. That was the good news. The harder topic was the "Who?"

Being childless became front and center in my mind. I tried to find the good in it. If I died on the table, no child would be left without a mom. Yet, emptiness lived in every cell of my body. If I did live through this, I was going to be an old maid, sitting in a rocking chair all by myself with no one to visit me.

I hated trying to be responsible.

As my parents and I left the attorney's office, our conversation floated around death and dying. I asked what their wishes were. *Do you want to be cremated? Or buried near Nana and Bumpa? What kind of flowers would you want on your coffin?* From the front seat of the car, my mother turned and smiled.

"I don't plan on going anywhere and don't want to talk about this anymore." *Bingo, Mom. Me, too.* I slid back into my seat and watched the world go by as my parents drove me home. We were not going to talk about dying. None of us were planning on going anywhere so the conversation was a moot point.

Sunday, February 8, 2009

This weekend was the Going Away Party for my nipples with Crack.

Friday morning, I hopped out of bed, packed my bags—complete with lacy lingerie—and kissed Punky and Mazey good-bye. "It's only one night. I'll be back tomorrow." They stared at me with sad, lonely eyes as I walked out the door and made my escape.

Destination Mohonk was two hours away; plenty of time to act like a sales person and answer phone calls and coordinate fabrics and negotiate discounts as I drove the Thruway. The conversations clicked away and the wheels of my mini-van kept moving me forward. Finally, cell service died. *Thank God.* My breathing slowed down. The stress of work started to fade. Snow-covered pinetrees lined the winding narrow passage that led up the mountain. The stone-built Victorian castle slowly came into view, complete with turrets and rustic porches. Rock formations rose majestically above the ice-covered lake on the left and the view of the valley on the right went on for miles. The fire pit in the nearby skating pavilion had puffs of smoke escaping its chimney and a couple held hands as they snowshoed across the fields.

The valet graciously took my keys and bags as I floated into the dark wood-paneled reception area. The smell of a fire hung in the air. Burgundy paisley carpet ran the length of the hallway, with Victorian sofas and chairs placed sporadically throughout.

"Bethany Parks. Two people. One night." I beamed at the receptionist.

"Room 214," she replied, handing me the key. "Up the stairs. To the left."

The room was smaller than shown on the website. Pink- and green-flowered wallpaper and a high-rise mattress were probably supposed to give the feel of being in fairy tale land. I'd kind of been hoping for the luxury suite that had its own fireplace and Jacuzzi with a view overlooking the valley, but at the moment, that room was outside of my tight budget.

I laid on the bed and watched the snowflakes drop from the sky through the tiny window. Crack would be late. He hadn't told me he would be, but I just knew. History. It was part of what I was willing to settle for in order to fill that needy, insecure feeling inside of me.

I drifted in and out of a nap, finally awaking with a clear thought. *The spa!* The spa was calling my name. I headed to the newly renovated portion of the castle and, as I walked through the elegant cherry doors, my soul was lifted. The light smell of lavender permeated the space. Hilary—a slender, exotic blond with a British accent—led me to the locker room and pointed out the amenities. Soft, white terry cloth robes with matching slippers; tall, thin glasses of water with pretty little lemon slices in them; and multiple options for an afternoon full of self-indulgence… a steam room, a sauna, a pool, a solarium, and an outdoor hot tub.

The first stop was the steam room. It was like sitting inside a hot cloud. I laid back on the wooden planks, allowing my thoughts to wonder.

I'm so lucky to be here. Life is so good. This moment is magical…. He's an asshole. What am I doing? I shouldn't be spending this money. I should be working. I should be returning

phone calls and selling chairs. He's such an asshole. Breathe.
Breathe. Breathe. Surgery. Chemo. Radiation. Breathe.

Tears began flowing freely from my eyes like the sweat from my pores.

I needed to do something else.

A natural stone walkway led outside to the spacious patio. An inviting plume of steam headed towards the heavens from the circular stone hot tub. I submerged myself in the heat of the water, allowing it to caress my body and my soul. Snowflakes fell on my face as sweat trickled from my forehead. Sounds of branches creaking under the weight of heavy white snow filled the air. The scent of pine filled my senses. Seconds turned to minutes. Minutes turned to hours as I continued to breathe and release and let go. *In. Out. In. Out.* I was floating in the hands of the Big Guy up above. I was being taken care of. I was okay... until I wasn't.

What time is it? Where is Crack? I thought. *What about my party? He's such an inconsiderate bastard. I should just leave.*

But I didn't. Instead, I let anxiety become my companion and headed back to the room, settling into bed with a not-so-great book.

Finally, Crack graced me with his presence.

"I'm sorry I'm late."

"Yeah," I replied matter-of-factly. "It's okay."

I was so passive-aggressive, and with zero ability to match words with my feelings.

My pain was outweighed by my needs. My angst evaporated like the water in the pool. My eyes were full and my body screamed for attention.

He knew it. He knew exactly what to do. Our bodies spoke the same language. Somehow, I thought this meant that our souls were on the same wavelength.

Afterwards, I showered to help wash away the uneasiness in my stomach. I silently watched the etched body pull on a pressed white shirt. His strong hands deftly worked around the dainty buttons. A black cashmere jacket and soft Levis were the finishing touches.

Please just let this go on forever. He's so handsome. And he's here with me. And I just love everything about him.

He opened the door for me as we headed towards the dining room for our seven o'clock reservations. As we descended the majestic, wooden staircase, my "knight in shining armor" suddenly went pale. He stopped on the landing.

"I don't feel good," he blurted out as he slumped onto a bench.

"You don't feel good? Are you going to be sick? Is there anything I can get for you?" I knelt in front of him, concerned for his health.

"No. It's okay. I just don't think I can go to dinner. I'm going back to the room to lay down."

Befuddled. Torn. Sad. There went the dream. There went the goodbye party. There went my hope that this was something that it wasn't. I headed to the dining room alone and stood at the hostess station alone. I scanned the menu for something that would fill the emptiness inside me. A scallop puff pastry something-or-other and a small salad.

"Please deliver it to room 214," I said to the tuxedo-clad waiter. "Thank you."

It was a shameful walk down the long hallway towards the stairs that led to the second floor. Couples walked past, hand in hand, headed to dinner. A crackling fire was going in the sitting room and an elderly, white-haired couple sat side-by-side reading their books, sipping tea. A family had just returned from snowshoeing, three young children in tow, all bundled up in pink and green snow suits and hats, with rosy-red cheeks, squealing in delight about the skating rink and the snow.

I made my way to the room, situated myself in a wing-back chair with my shitty book, and watched Crack sleep.

Seething inside, my inner voice screamed, "*What about me? What about me? Don't you know what I am going through? Are you really sick? I don't fucking believe you. I think you just got scared and didn't want to do anything as intimate as having dinner with me. Fuck you.*"

As usual, I didn't kick him out. I didn't leave. I just felt like shit for the whole night. We parted ways in the morning and I swore I was done. I swore it.

Wednesday, February 25, 2009

The pre-op area on surgery day was like a holding pattern at the airport. Each patient was waiting for takeoff. My parents sat next me, my mom holding my hand, as Dr. Kauffman came whipping into the bay dressed in jeans, a designer jacket, and the latest and greatest chocolate leather satchel. She sipped her latte and explained more about the procedure—stuff I didn't really want to hear.

"What are you doing after this?" I wondered aloud.

"My regular Wednesday night yoga class."

Bitch! *Didn't she know she was about to screw me all up?* I took a deep breath. I got it, though. Although I resented the fact that her life would carry on, I realized that it was exactly how it should be. I didn't want her to stay in my world for too long—just long enough to remove any remaining potentially cancerous cells from my body.

As we chatted, I was pleasantly surprised to learn Dr. Kauffman was training to do a triathlon and raising money for cancer research. I let out a mental sigh.

"How's the swimming going?" I asked.

"It's not my strongest sport. But I have a coach and I practice a lot."

"A coach? Who's your coach? Don't tell me. Coach Bonnie, right?"

Her face lit up. "YES! Coach Bonnie. How did you know?"

"I did the same thing. She's awesome, right? What a great teacher. I sucked at swimming, too. Don't worry—it gets better, kind of."

We bantered back and forth about drills as I lay on the gurney waiting to have my breasts removed. There was now a personal link between my surgeon and I. I was sure I would receive special treatment—my delusions of being terminally unique ran rampant even in these situations.

Dr. Kauffman excused herself to change and prep for surgery. My gaze shifted to the nurse anesthetist standing to my left.

I adamantly announced my wishes. "I don't want to remember anything and I don't want any pain when I wake up." As soon as the snotty sounding words left my mouth, I realized that most likely I was not the first person who had said this to her. Her reply was straightforward and direct.

"It's a pretty big surgery. For me to tell you there will be no pain is unrealistic."

It was the destruction of my denial yet again. Pretty big surgery, but no guarantees—they did this all the time; yoga at 6:30. Normal.

Both my parents kissed me on the cheek as I was wheeled away, the anesthesia slowly dripping into my system.

A couple hours later, I found myself semi-conscious with bright lights jolting my senses awake. Mom and Dad were at the foot of the bed as I opened my eyes. Marie sat in the chair next to me.

"Everything went well," Dad said. "Sounds like she got everything."

"Oh good." I smiled at him this time. The anesthesiologist had been wrong. There was no pain.

Mom kissed my cheek and pointed out the window to the snow falling against the black sky. "There's a big storm coming in. We're supposed to get a foot of snow. We want to get on the road and beat the traffic." They were getting older, and worried about these things now.

I nodded. "Go. You should go."

"Are you sure you're okay?" Dad asked.

I located the red morphine pump button and smiled at Marie.

"I'm good. Don't worry. Drive safe. I love you."

Daddy kissed my cheek. "We'll see you tomorrow. Love you. Sleep tight." My father held my mother's hand as they left the room.

Marie pulled her chair up next to me and smiled.

"I brought the princess tiara thing. It's in the bag over there." I pointed to the corner. "We have to take a picture. It's part of the adventure."

I loved my friend Marie. She was one of the most organized, predictable, responsible people I had ever met. She knew I was crazy. And she liked me anyway.

I smiled as big as possible as she placed the sparkling, fake rhinestone crown on my head and snapped a shot, then turned the phone to show me the image.

The oxygen tube floating across my face was not attractive. My hair was greasy. I looked a little gray.

"Oh shit." Laughter barreled from my body. "I look like shit."

Marie's small frame shook with glee. "Yeah, you do."

"Send it to Crack. You gotta' send it to Crack," I said.

"Are you sure?" she laughed. "Are you really sure you want to do that?"

Marie was my conscience. When my brain didn't work, she was who I went to. I trusted her implicitly.

"Yes. Yes. We have to. It's too funny not to." My drug-induced self was relentless. She punched in the number and sent away. I don't remember if I ever got a response.

My friend and I chatted away as if we were sitting in a coffee shop. Actually, I rambled non-stop and I think she just listened. It was the drugs. I liked to blame everything on the drugs.

Eventually, the buzz lifted and my body started to feel the pain. Marie had been in this bed before. She knew what this was like, and she was my coach. I loved her like a sister.

We exchanged a big air hug and she headed out the door to be with her family. "Thank you so much for coming. I love, love, love you!" I yelled to my friend as she left the room.

"I love you, too!" she yelled back.

I hit the little morphine pump button and floated back to Neverland.

Sleeping through the night was easy with narcotics. Pushing that red button became an immediate reflex when any twinge of pain hit my body. *No pain. I don't want pain. Drugs. I want drugs.*

As the sun rose and light entered the bland hospital room, I didn't want to be a part of day. *Red button. Pump. Pump.* The warm, relaxing feeling infiltrated my blood stream—through my arms to my fingers, through my legs to my toes. My eyelids closed as I was carried back to my happy place away from all of this nonsense.

By one o'clock the drugs wore off. My mindset was different this time. I wiggled my toes and my fingers and everything worked. I didn't really want to stay in this antiseptic, ugly room for the day. I wanted to get away from all of this, literally. It was eleven o'clock in the morning and I was ready to go home. The nurses had checked on me and assured me that I would be released shortly. I hoisted myself to the side of the bed and got dressed, working around the plastic drains that were coming out of both of my armpits and the corset-type wrap strangling my chest.

Aimee texted me at noon. "What room are you in?"

"307."

Within minutes, my red-headed roommate was walking through the door.

"I'm ready to go home," I promptly announced to her.

"Really? I was just coming to visit. You can go home today?"

"Yep. Like now. We just have to check out. How are the roads?"

She was startled and surprised. "How do you feel?"

"Good. Good. Let's go."

"I can't believe you're going home today."

"That's what they said. I felt like shit this morning, but I can move now. Let's go before they change their minds."

A nurse entered the room, I signed the release forms, grabbed my stack of paperwork with the list of meds to pick up, and a guy with a wheelchair transported me to the outside world. *Free. Fresh air. New snow.*

I gingerly situated myself in the front seat of Aimee's Jeep. "Thank you for coming to visit. I'm so happy you showed up."

Strapping on the seatbelt was not going to happen. I didn't care if it was illegal or reckless. I wasn't doing it.

"I didn't think I was taking you home. I figured you'd be here for a while."

"Nope. Guess not. It's probably an insurance thing." I dialed my dad's cell phone.

"Hi, honey. How you feel?"

"Hey, Dad. We're on our way home."

"WHAT? You're coming home? Now?"

"Yep. Aimee came to visit and we're on our way. They let me out," I giggled.

"Wow. Okay. Well, we'll see you soon. Drive safe."

The roads had been cleared, but snow covered the landscape with a bright, clean layer of white. I rested my head on the seat and let my friend negotiate the streets and highways and carry me home.

As we pulled into the driveway, I smiled at the little green house where I lived. It wasn't magnificent or fancy or designer anything. It was ordinary and comfortable and perfect, a one-floor ranch on a road full of the same. Aimee helped me open the car door as we made our way inside. Mom and Dad looked at me as if they had seen a ghost.

"I can't believe they let you out." Mom sounded annoyed as she sipped her coffee. "You would think they would have kept you for another day just to make sure you're okay. Stupid doctors."

"I'm fine, Mom. Really, I am. I wanted to be home." I kissed her on the cheek. The non-descript green velour recliner in the small family room was calling my name. It was neatly situated in front of the TV and surrounded by pillows, stuffed animals, and books.

"You want a cup of coffee?"

"Sure. That would be great." My bruised body and battered emotions slipped into the comfort zone. My family and friends had entered caretaker mode and I had entered patient mode.

My new oncologist, Dr. Miller, the one who worked at the hospital with the nice bistro, called within hours. I picked up the remote and muted *Law and Order: SVU*. "We need to schedule your chemo sessions." I hadn't heard the pleasantries before or after that statement.

"Now? We need to schedule them now?" My whining had begun. I just wanted a hiatus from treatment. Unfortunately, he didn't care what I wanted. He was in production mode and I was inside the healthcare machine.

"We need to allow your incisions to heal. A couple of weeks. At that point, we'll start your treatments. Once every two weeks, with interim visits for Neulasta shots and bloodwork. The sooner we start the process, the sooner it will be over."

Fuck him.

During our initial consultation, I had negotiated a small but significant detail regarding my treatment. I would be bringing my own treatment chair to the hospital. It was part of the deal. *I let you poison my body in your hospital. You let me bring my own chair.* The premier treatment chair, the one with heat and massage built in. No uncomfortable, cheap, metal, cold chairs for this girl. Not a chance.

"March 18th. I got it. That's the chemo start date. I'll have my chair dropped off, okay? Please let the nurses know." He agreed.

Dad set off to the pharmacy to pick up my new coping mechanisms, a.k.a. drugs while Mom and I settled in for the afternoon television shows. After Ellen, they hit the road for the three hour ride home. They weren't ones for staying long.

Thursday, February 26, 2009

The green recliner/makeshift-sleeping surface in the family room and I did not always get along. Last night was probably the worst.

My chair wasn't hugging me like I wanted it to. I tenderly tossed and turned, and tried to find a comfortable spot. Zero luck.

Meanwhile, my kitchen counter had become a small pharmacy of tiny orange bottles with white lids—complete with painkillers, anti-nausea meds, and sleeping pills. I popped a couple of Ambien and headed back to my chair with the hope of drifting off to a restful place. It didn't work. I tried to read a trashy romance novel about the perfect cowboy who owned racehorses, looked great in jeans, and was struggling with intimacy. That didn't work. I finished a Sudoku puzzle and started another one, and then got aggravated with counting to nine.

As I tried to count sheep, my stomach started to move and make a loud gurgling noise. I closed my eyes and felt my breath come in and out of my nostrils, making every attempt to ignore the rumbling and tumbling inside my belly. *Breathe In. Breathe Out.* Rhythmic breathing led to relentless panting and sweat spilling from every pore in my body. Aimee was sleeping on the sofa next to me, her breathing consistent and relaxed. She was probably having dreams of riding her Harley through rolling hills on a beautiful summer evening and I was sitting in a gross green velour recliner being pissed that she was breathing so calmly. I was torn between screaming, "Shut the fuck up," and trying to keep my stomach from barreling out of my throat.

By one o'clock in the morning, I had lost the battle with my stomach and become intimate with the toilet. For an hour, I felt cold porcelain pressed against my skin. As my internal organs rearranged themselves inside my body, I worried if the stitches holding my chest together would rupture and blood would splatter all over the floor. I heaved again. My body was doubled over the sink and my fingers gripped the edge for stability.

"Are you okay?" Aimee called out to me from the sofa.

I tried to respond, but instead fell over the toilet vomiting. After each round, I would put my hands to my chest, making sure my body was all in one piece. My head pounded and my insides felt like they were now my outsides. Tears dripped down my face. I didn't want to do this. I didn't want any part of this.

I tried to gain some composure and get back to a place where I could breathe.

Aimee came up behind me and rubbed my back. Minutes passed, and finally the sickness subsided. "Thank you for being here," I muttered, trembling.

The green chair wasn't so inviting afterwards, so Aimee helped me to the living room sofa, but I couldn't get comfortable, so I moved back to the green recliner. It was futile. I wandered through the house, staring out each window, looking at pictures, touching books. Relief escaped me for the night. Eventually, the morning sun finally appeared and a new day became the happy ending to my sleepless night.

Sunday, March 1, 2009

Crack was here last night. He actually showed up on time. I greeted him at the door with a sad smile and a twist in my heart, hoping that he really cared about me and this wasn't just a sympathy visit. He carefully wrapped his arms around me and I laid my head on his chest, sobbing quietly. I couldn't lift my arms up to hug him back.

When I could breathe again, he held me out and looked at me. "How are you?"

"I'm okay. It's just hard. In so many ways."

"Tell me about it."

We ate peanut butter and jelly sandwiches, and I told him about surgery, recovery, and feeling helpless—and when I couldn't talk about it anymore, I pulled him into the family room and plopped onto the sofa.

"I have drains coming out of me. Can I show them to you?"

Crack was an EMT. He had lived in Iraq for a year during the war and had seen everything. He nodded without hesitation.

I unbuttoned my shirt to expose large strips of white gauze tightly wrapped around my chest. Half-inch tubing was stitched into each armpit, and it ran the length of each arm to small plastic bubbles that held bloody, oozy fluid. His expression was not one of shock. It was one of medical awareness.

I looked at him as if I was looking into his soul. "Thank you for not being scared of me." I leaned over and kissed him. He held my face between his hands and kissed me back. My body reacted to him as it always did. Gently, he laid me back, kissed me softly, and allowed me the pleasures of being a woman. I was relieved to find that everything still worked. My sexuality hadn't been totally compromised. Afterwards, he opened his arms and let me snuggle in against his body. My drains pulled at my skin. The wrap made my breathing difficult. But when he asked if I was comfortable and gave me a quick hug, all pain vanished. We took a quick nap and, before I knew it, he was gone.

Maybe when I become a big girl and turn forty-two, I'll start to understand men. Shit. I'm just an ass. I know Crack comes and goes. I know he doesn't stay. I know there are other women. Yet, I can't resist him. What is wrong with me?

As I walked down the hallway toward my room, I stood in front of my War Wall complete with appointments and sayings. At the top of the wall were two words. *Peace and Serenity*. Crack was not getting me there. What a surprise.

I knew there were other options for me. I knew I could go without him. I knew I was capable and strong and sexy and amazing and loveable. Or at least that's what my friends and therapist constantly told me. I wanted to believe it. I wanted to think all those positive things about myself. I wanted to think I deserved great things in my life.

Then I realized that maybe I was using him as much as he was using me. *Going to lose breasts? Need service? Call Crack.*

The duct tape and gauze that were holding my chest together hurt more than the stitches. There were times during the day when I struggled to get air into my lungs. It was like a truck had parked itself on my torso. Then, while Aimee and I sat watching TV together one afternoon, I felt an itch in the lower left part of my chest. It was an itch that was not going away. It felt like it would eat my skin alive.

"I gotta' take this shit off, Aim," I blurted out. "Will you help me?"

We stood in the bathroom with a pair of scissors, a sink full of hot water, and a ton of apprehension. Aimee cut the tape, unraveled the gauze, and pulled off the packing. I stood in front of the mirror staring at my naked chest. Black stitches were sewn in the form of a V. There were no more nipples. My chest was flat, but with a slight raise, which was obviously the expanders. Another incision had been made near the top of my collarbone where the chemo port had been installed.

"It's not that bad," Aimee said reassuringly, offering me a comforting smile.

I burst into sobs.

Aimee used a warm wet washcloth and cleaned off my chest. We then gently replaced the soft white camisole around my body and went back to the sofa and the TV.

Saturday, March 7, 2009

Nothing was normal. I had a feeling that normal, as I knew it, would never be the same again.

Normal is a crazy word. I think it should be banned. It's judgmental. *Delete. Done.*

A good word is *patience*. When this whole process began, I contemplated the meaning of the word, and now I try to live it every day. I learned how to sit for a couple of days to let my body finish draining and start to heal. I learned to knit a little better. I learned about napping. I learned about letting myself rest. This really was about the journey, not the destination. This was about meeting new people, spending time with people I already knew and learning about their lives, not taking my life for granted, and embracing the process. Somehow, this all reminded me of some pretty basic life lessons. Love, patience and faith.

I needed to practice saying, "I *am* okay." Not, "I am *going* to be okay." It had to be present tense: "At this moment, all is right with me."

Thursday was my first appointment with Dr. Murphy, my plastic surgeon. My parents came in the night before and would be staying with me for moral support. Dad drove me to the doctor's office since my mobility was still limited and I hated the idea of seatbelts.

"Bethany?" the nurse Maureen called my name, and then she escorted me to the exam room. I'd assumed this would be one of those "Let's look and see" type of visits. I'd been wrong.

"I'm going to remove the tape around your incisions and take out the stitches."

"ARE YOU KIDDING ME?" I exclaimed, horrified. "I don't even want you to touch me!" My chest felt like a truck had run over it, and she wanted to talk about tweezers and scissors and pulling out the stitches!

Maureen smiled a sweet smile, clearly unfazed by my outburst, and replied, "It feels that way because the nerves have been cut."

I didn't really care why it felt like it did; I just didn't want anyone, especially someone with sharp utensils, near me. She didn't care. Reluctantly, I reclined back on the exam table. Maureen laid the cold, stainless steel tools on my chest and yanked and pulled at the tape that held me together. She took scissors, snipped at the seams on my chest, and plucked and pulled the thread from my sternum. I bit down on my lip to keep from screaming out of pain and horror. Piece by piece, the black stitches were removed. It was a mini version of a Frankenstein movie.

Finally, we were done. Or so I thought.

"Dr. Murphy will start the fill process next," Maureen said, laying a gentle hand on my arm.

Shit, there's more? Wasn't this enough?

I stared at the gray laminate countertop as Maureen neatly arranged the next set of tools: a syringe with a three-inch needle on it along with a vile of liquid. This was bizarre, like out of a horror movie or something. Some mad scientist doctor trying to recreate a person with needles and magic potions.

Dr. Murphy entered the room with a big smile and a light-hearted greeting. "Well, well, let's see what we have here today. How do you feel?"

Still biting down on my lip, I made eye contact and just nodded. As she put on blue latex gloves, she announced,

"I'm going to take this little magnet here and roll it along your chest. There are metal valves in your expanders, and when I find them, I'll mark them with a big X."

Here we were again, I thought, *making marks with Sharpie markers on my chest.*

"After that, I'm going to inject thirty CCs of saline into each side. There will be pressure as your muscles start to expand in order to accommodate the growth."

I tried to breathe, and replied, "You are going to stick those needles into me? Isn't there a better way?"

"Oh, don't worry. You'll get used to this. This process will become ordinary after a few times."

She's full of shit.

As I clutched Maureen's hand, I turned my head away. It was too bizarre, too weird. My chest started to feel the pressure from the inside out.

A few seconds later, Dr. Murphy beamed at me. "Okay. That's one side. Let's do the other one and then you are out of here."

Another needle. Another squeamish glance away from what was going on. Another moment of pressure to reshape my body.

"All done."

It was getting harder to say "thank you" after situations like this, just as it was getting harder to keep things in perspective. But I had to believe that I was getting closer to being healthy. There had to be a silver lining someplace.

Dad drove me home, listening to me bitch the whole way. Mom had whipped up her specialty—ham and cheese sandwiches on white bread with wavy potato chips on paper plates. We watched *Ellen* and eventually Mom and Dad headed home, leaving me to sit with my laptop, my cats, and the TV.

Tuesday, March 17, 2009

Chemo started today. Happy almost St. Patrick's Day to me.

The anxiety leading up to the actual event was more disturbing than the event itself. Even the word sounded bad. *Chemo.* I was imagining this horrible process in which I would turn gray in a matter of hours. The reality is that chemo is just an IV drip. It's simply four hours sitting in a chair while poison runs through my veins and supposedly kills whatever cancer cells are left in my body. No big deal.

The chemo suite—or "oncology suite" as it's professionally termed—is a long hallway with four private rooms on either side, which lead to an open area.

As I walked the white linoleum floor, I peeked curiously into each room.

In each was a bed, a good quality guest chair covered in green vinyl, and a cabinet with a TV in it. The beds had people in them, too—bald people covered in blankets, mostly sleeping, with worried-looking people sitting in the chairs next to them. I reached the check-in counter and was greeted by a smiling, bubbly young woman whose nametag said Libby.

"Hi. I'm Bethany," I stated matter-of-factly. "This is my friend, Aimee."

"It's so nice to meet you," Libby greeted me as if we were at a chamber of commerce dinner function. "If you would have a seat, we'll be with you in just a minute." She pointed to the waiting room opposite her.

Aimee and I glanced at each other and the common area full of velour-covered La-Z-Boy recliners. They'd probably been purchased at the local household furniture store. The chairs were full of old, bald people who looked really sick—like, dying sick.

That's not me. That's not going to be me. I promise.

There were IV poles, blankets, and *The Price is Right* blaring from the corner television.

Aimee and I leaned against the wall in the hallway while we waited for my designated seat. Within minutes, an attractive brunette dressed in scrubs approached us.

"Hi. I'm Beth. You must be Bethany." She'd directed the statement at me. Probably because I looked the most terrified.

"Yup. That's me. Did the doctor tell you I'm having a treatment chair delivered this week?"

"Oh yes. He did. We will find a spot for it." That made me happy at least. "Let's get this started."

I was introduced to Nurse Rose, Nurse May Lou, and about six others, all of them equally cherry and friendly as I was seated with the sick people. Bob Barker on the TV asked the next contestant how much she thought a box of Rice-A-Roni was. Most of the people hooked up to IV bags looked to be sleeping. No one was smiling. It was dreary. I looked at Aimee for some support.

"How much is Rice-A-Roni?" I asked.

"I don't eat that shit." She smirked. My friend preferred to cook her own. Packaged products weren't really her thing.

Beth returned with a tray full of needles and antiseptic wipes and bandages. Within minutes, she was sticking a needle in the port located near my collarbone. The needle was attached to a tube that eventually led to fluid hanging on the IV pole. There was no poking and prodding at the veins in my arms. Technology had improved over the years, and these port things were the latest and greatest invention in the world of chemo. I leaned back and watched as the fluid dripped slowly into the tube and then into me. The first bag was something like Benadryl to prevent allergic reactions, then came the steroids to help with the inflammation and then came the heavy hitters of Adriamycin and Cyclophosphamide (also known as AC). The pump would make it's pumping noise and then it would beep when it was done and the nurse would change each bag out- one by one. Overall, it was a very boring process—one that I didn't plan on getting used to.

Aimee and I watched TV, read magazines, napped. Ding. Ding. Ding. We had a winner from the TV. Middle America housewife wins trip to Puerto Rico. Ding. Ding. Ding.

Wednesday, March 18, 2009

This morning, I woke up and went to meet some friends. I needed to get myself out of bed, out of the house, and especially out of my head. I had a group of friends who got together every day for coffee—just like the old people you see in the greasy spoon diners. They didn't let me take pity on myself or start to play the victim role. Everyone had their own shit going on: loss of jobs, challenging relationships, physical ailments, tragedies of all shapes and sizes. We talked about gratitude, helping others, and taking things one step at a time. I needed to stay attached to these old bitties.

By nine a.m., I was home and needed a nap. Aimee was at work. Punky and Mazey wrapped themselves around me as my head hit the pillow. It was still early in the day, and I was already back in bed. It was tough to accept, but this would be my new life—at least for now. It was twenty-four hours after my first chemo treatment and the drugs were kicking in. Unwillingly, I would have to accept the fact that my body was going to wear out faster than it used to.

My parents drove in from Binghamton again. They arrived around lunchtime, and though they tried not to show it, "DOOM" was plastered all over their faces as they stepped into the house. Their fears over chemo and cancer were never really discussed. They were just manifested in facial expressions, body language, and often odd tones in their voices.

"Hello? We're here!" Mom's voice had a slight catch in it; not like her usual bellowing self.

"Hi." I hugged my mom as tightly as I could without creating pain in my chest.

"How was the ride?" I asked Dad as he wrapped his arms around me.

"Good. No traffic. Nice day. How are you feeling?" he asked as Mom started to unpack bags of food in the kitchen.

"I'm good. Just a little tired. Mom. Mom!" I shouted to her. "What's with all the food?"

"I just wanted to make sure you had some stuff around." Mom had never really been a big cook. Her efforts at caretaking included homemade macaroni and cheese, a bag of oranges, and boatloads of cold cuts. Aimee would be happy with the full refrigerator, but personally I was worried what all this extra food and less movement would do to my already un-fit figure.

Mom and Dad stayed for one night, long enough for them to see that I was alive, play a couple of hands of cards, and watch TV for a few hours. Low maintenance. We were in low maintenance mode.

Wednesday, March 25, 2009

It had been just one week since the first round of chemo, and as soon as I found a few strands of hair falling out, I scheduled THE SHAVING. I was *not* going to watch clumps of red hair fill the drain of my shower or see a nest on my pillow every morning. I wasn't going to wait for this hair loss thing to happen. I wasn't going to be a victim to this side effect.

My chemo hospital had a sweet little salon situated right next to the waterfall in the waiting room. I'm not sure *salon* was the right word for it, though, because no hair styling actually went on there. The room was full of wigs, scarves, and knit hats. The chair was the normal hair styling chair: black leather with the up-and-down pneumatic mechanism, appropriately placed in front of a wall of mirrors.

My friend Alison had agreed to be my support person for the day. She stood in the corner as I perched myself in the chair and smiled at the beautician.

Karen and Vickie were part of the oncology staff at the hospital and had helped plan the Going Away Party for my hair. It would be a small-scale event. No balloons or cakes. Just a couple of positive people trying to make the most of a rather difficult situation.

"Oh, you are going to be so beautiful bald," Karen said.

"Your blue eyes are just going to pop," added Vickie.

"I bet you say that to all the girls," I laughed.

The buzz-cutter made lines into my thick red hair. Strip by strip, tufts of hair fell to the ground as Alison,

Karen, Vickie, and I had our mini-event in the oncology hair studio.

It was just hair. It would grow back. Vanity be damned!

I had already detached from my physicality. The loss of body parts had been the jumping-off point. The hair loss was just another opportunity to practice being more than a body or a face. Me. The person. That was more important. I was still the fun-loving, easy-going person who I had always been… just minus a few physical things.

After every last strand had been shaved away, the hairstylist turned me to face the mirror. Within minutes, my hair had gone from gorgeous auburn to sparse, prickly, quarter-inch stubs. But as I looked in the mirror, I was happy to note that I did not have an egg-shaped skull. It was round. A nice, round head. There were no defining indents or canyons or craters that I could see.

"Nice head," Karen said.

I let out a deep laugh. There would undoubtedly be some funny ways to frame this. It was not a complete alien staring back at me. The face was actually kind of cute and impish looking. My eyes were indeed bigger now. The skin was whiter. The neck was longer. Strength emanated from the person in the mirror.

It wasn't such a bad thing.

Sunday, March 29, 2009

Aimee was a Godsend. Having a roommate had never been top of my priority list when I'd become single, but sometimes things just work out.

Today, Aimee took me on my first motorcycle ride of the year. I got to wear my new leather coat and chaps, and my skullcap that was covered in stickers with inappropriate sayings like, "There's nothing like a 700# vibrator." We wrapped my head in a long orange scarf and placed the little skull cap snuggly on top. Then we saddled up on our iron horses and headed out into the wilderness.

Down back country roads and around sweeping turns in the middle of the woods, I felt the wind against my face. It was brisk and snappy. The vibration of the machine moved through my hands, my arms, and every inch of my body. My chest was tight, but the rest of my soul was fluid. Aimee led the way, flowing with the road, so comfortable in her seat. As I followed her, I was aware of all the things the Big Guy did for me when I couldn't do them for myself. I thanked Him for my friend Aimee and for the freedom she had given me. *Freedom.* Freedom from fear, from judgment, and from cancer. If only for a few hours.

Tuesday, March 31, 2009

Chemo treatment number two. I knew the drill. *Check in with the receptionist. Have blood drawn. Go upstairs to see the doctor. Work on a jigsaw puzzle to pass the time in the waiting room. Get instructions. Head back downstairs and begin the chemo process.*

On this particular day, I showed up with a bag of buttons—smiley-face buttons to be exact. How can you not love the little yellow roundness and the simplicity of that smile? It just screams *happy*! My goal for retirement was to be a greeter at Wal-Mart and hand out smiley-face stickers for a living. But, for now, I settled for handing out smiley-face buttons to the receptionist, the nurses, the doctors, and anyone who would look at me. I would not be deterred.

Karen Cook, the oncology social worker—a.k.a. the on-the-spot therapist for cancer patients having mental breakdowns—showed up as I was waiting in the lobby to be called for my chemo drip. I had the distinct feeling that she knew I was a bit off-center. There wasn't necessarily a green neon light blinking LUNATIC plastered on my forehead, but there was a general vibe.

"Hey, chick," she said, beaming. "What's going on?"

"Oh nothing," I replied. "Want a smiley face?"

"Only you." She smiled as she pinned the yellow circle to her shirt.

"My chair is here, right?" I asked.

"Let's check it out." She walked me into the infusion center and asked if a chair had been delivered.

"*You're* the one with *the* chair?" asked Nurse Rose, wide-eyed.

"Yep. That's me. I do chairs. Want a smiley face?"

Head Nurse Mary Lou asked, "Are you leaving The Chair here? We love it."

"Oh, yeah. It's staying. But only as long as I'm here."

My heart did a few somersaults. Maybe I could actually sell a few chairs while going through this ordeal. *I should visit the purchasing department after they pull the needles out of my chest. If I remember.*

Work was still a big part of my brain.

Treatment room number six. That's where The Chair was located. The treatment chair with high-end vinyl, a soft little headrest, and heat and massage built into the seat—or, as I liked to call it, the throne. Treatment room number six had a wall of windows, a TV opposite the chair, and a few mismatched guest chairs shoved along the wall. But The Chair was the centerpiece. I hoped it was comfortable.

I went into the room and unpacked my bag of important stuff: my laptop, my phone, hard candy to fight off the metallic taste that would soon develop in my mouth, a Sudoku book, and a few water bottles. You would think I was staying for a week, but after the first time I'd been there, I had drawn up a list of stuff to bring to keep me preoccupied.

Nurse Rose arrived with the tray of paraphernalia needed to get the party started: needles, wipes, gauze, tape, and bags of poison.

"So, you sell chairs?" she asked.

"Yeah, that's kind of what I do. I started to focus on the healthcare industry in the last couple of years, never really thinking that I would need to use one of these things. And then, ta-dah! Here I am. Since there was a sample hanging around in my garage, I figured I might as well bring it here and do some testing on it."

Rose told me about a patient who'd been in the day before—an elderly lady, very frail and in the later stages of the disease. Typically, she would lie in a bed during her infusion—it was the only place she felt comfortable—but yesterday not even the bed had worked for her. Her entire body had ached. The nurses had decided to try something different, so they'd brought her into treatment room number six, gently placed her in the chair, turned on the heat and massage, tucked her in with a warm blanket, and left her. A half hour later, she'd been fast asleep.

Maybe chairs really do make a difference, I thought as Rose finished her story.

The cynic in me had been a bit nervous about using my sample. What if it wasn't really that comfortable? How would I ever sell this thing with a straight face again? I was a good salesperson, but not that good. I couldn't lie. I *wouldn't* lie. But, fortunately, I didn't need to.

After Rose started the IV drip and left the room, I turned on the heat and massage, plugged in my laptop, and enjoyed the ability to do quotes for conference tables from treatment room number six. It was a mini-vacation from the rat race of the outside world.

When the chemo started to take hold and my body succumbed to the drugs, I moved into a semi-comatose state while my brain started to wander, thinking back to when I'd been married.

When I'd left my husband two years before, I'd had no idea where it would take me.

All I knew was that I couldn't stay anymore. It had been seventeen years, and I was not a good wife. Even with tons of therapy. I couldn't connect some of the dots in my head. I couldn't understand why I wasn't content. We had new cars, new TVs, and new furniture. There was a boat, bikes, a pool, and a beautiful yard. But I always wanted more. I wanted more attention, more adventure… just more, more, more. That thirteen-year-old free spirit was alive and well inside of me. I couldn't pretend anymore. I couldn't pretend to be a good wife when I wasn't. I couldn't pretend to be happy when, inside, my soul was deflating. So, I left and ended up in a friend's fully furnished house in Saratoga. It was in a good location, cheap and clean. The down side? The owners came back to the house during track season each summer. Saratoga was home to the oldest horserace track in the country, and each year from mid-July until Labor Day, the town became a hustle and bustle of activity that came complete with the rich and famous of the equestrian world. Many locals vacated their homes to allow for seasonal rentals. My situation was just reversed. I rented all year, but needed to leave when the horses came to town. Just a minor bump in the road.

My brain wandered regularly, and one question that had started to haunt me in every waking moment reappeared.

What do I want to do?

With the track season in the not so distant future, I needed to come up with a plan. What would I do that year? The thought for the day was to rent a RV and put it on a lake for six weeks, from the middle of July to the end of August. Or I could buy a house. Or I could be a real nomad, wandering from place to place. But I had to do radiation every day. That needed to be part of the plan. I had to be at least semi-responsible.

Monday, April 6, 2009

I hated cancer. Actually, I hated chemo more than the cancer. It was like an energy vampire with its fangs stuck deep into my entire life. I didn't want to talk to anyone. I didn't want to pet my cats. I didn't want to pretend that I was okay. I just wanted to sit and be alone. The only good news was that I was done with two cycles of chemo and there were only six more left. That was the good news.

One of the side effects of chemo was mouth sores. The medical term is herpes. Yeah, herpes is a by-product of chemo. I didn't even get to have sex and I still ended up with this venereal disease.

The Big Guy has a sick sense of humor.

I was losing steam. I had chemo crankiness. Nothing was right and there was a piece inside of me that was still in total denial about the status of my life.

Wednesday, April 8, 2009

A good day! HOORAH!

The doctors agreed that I could have chemo the following week. It was exciting news because it meant things were still on track. We were getting closer to the end. One day at a time. Moving forward. Cancer had become my new endurance sport. One foot in front of the other. One more simulator. One more mile. Keeping my eye on the end. It was just like training for a sport.

There was a fire in my belly today.

I started dreaming and making bucket lists of things to do with the rest of my life. I wanted to go back to St. John next winter. I wanted to do more triathlons. I wanted to be a better swimmer. I wanted to camp some and spend time outdoors. I wanted to write a book. I wanted to spend time with my nieces and nephews and my family. I wanted to be of service to people who needed help. I wanted to do something that mattered. I wanted to help people laugh. I wanted to be a better person.

Saturday, April 11, 2009

Spring had arrived. The robins were out. Snow was finally out of my yard. The tulips were up and coffee tasted good for the first time in a long time.

Punky and Mazey moved into my lap as the sun hit my face and I contemplated the day ahead.

My thought processes were often askew. I had been limiting myself by giving cancer and chemo and treatment more power than these things actually had. I had believed that I needed to be sedentary or so I told myself. Or maybe I really was tired and not lazy. Or maybe I was finding excuses not to exercise. Maybe I was stronger than I thought I was. I started asking questions of the doctor.

"Can I go swimming?" I asked the oncologists and plastic surgeons.

"Sure," they said.

"Can I run?"

"Sure. Why not?"

My stomach filled with butterflies. If the doctors said these things were all do-able, then what was my problem? Why was I not doing all the things that I used to do? My head was the problem. My head was limiting me. I was thinking too much, and that's never good. The most dangerous neighborhood was the one between my two ears.

I had to shake shit up. I was committed to getting outside and walking. Or going on the treadmill. Or a stationery bike. Or something. Walking into the gym would be difficult. The self-conscious part of being bald had been stopping me. Maybe the easiest thing was to walk out the door and get around the block at least. I had to shift into a different mindset in regards to my physical well-being.

Monday, April 13, 2009

Today was plastic surgeon day. I wished I was there for a face lift or a vanity boob job rather than the freak show associated with my chest. I was called into the exam room and did the standard process – remove top, add robe, climb on table to wait for the injections to begin. The nurse practitioner came in, laid out all the utensils, made the small talk and left me to wait for the doctor.

It was all so medical and sterile and freakish. Magnet to my chest. X marks the spot. Injection. Pressure. Other side. Breathe. Breathe. Breathe. I'm sure I tried to be nice with everyone in the office but I didn't really care anymore. I just wanted to be home in bed.

Tuesday, April 14, 2009

Chemo Treatment number three. I had the process under control now. My co-pilot for the day arrived at my house with bags of cookies, candies, and treats for the oncology team.

Sugar. Always a hit.

More smiley-face buttons were handed out.

Nurse Rose wandered in with her serving tray of needles, wet wipes, and tape.

"How's things?"

They always asked these types of questions, as if life was normal.

"F*** You" was what I wanted to say. But hey, she was only doing her job. And, basically, she was the one keeping me alive, so being nasty to her wasn't going to be the most beneficial move on my part.

"Fine," I answered.

She began talking about Easter dinner, spring weather, and chemo ports as she pushed back my shirt so she could access the metal valve near my collarbone. She rattled on as I looked at the budding tree out the window and the cars passing by. Tears slid down my cheek as scalloped potato recipes were passed around and she inserted the needle full of poison into my chest. It was bi-polar. This whole disease thing was bi-polar. One day good. One day a disaster.

"Okay, we're all set." She smiled.

"Awesome," I muttered.

The steroids and the anti-nausea meds wreaked havoc on my guts. My co-pilot and I ordered a cheeseburger *and* a chicken sandwich from the bistro down the hall. It was a food fest in treatment room six. Thank God, I'd picked a facility with room service.

Two weeks ago, I had shaved my head, and I'd since been wandering around town with a pretty cool military cut. But that wasn't really the end of the hair-cutting episode. The little black and white stubbles were now starting to fall out and leave a trail everywhere I looked, like a really bad case of dandruff. Someone suggested using a lint roller to keep these little buggers from making a mess all over the place. A glossy bald spot on the back of my head had also started to appear, probably from my pillow. It was time to take more action. I needed to become a true cue-ball.

I texted Crack. "Hey."

"Hey," my phone beeped back a few hours later.

I responded immediately, knowing I wouldn't have his attention for long. "Would you help me with something?"

"Sure. What?"

"Would you shave my head?"

A slight pause hung in the air as I stared at my Blackberry.

"Yes. When?"

Phew.

We scheduled a date and time, and within days, Crack was in my house again.

Well-worn Levis may be the softest texture in the universe. As I sat on the lid of my toilet, I couldn't keep my hands off the muscular legs that straddled me. He was as handsome as ever with a razor in one hand and a warm washcloth in the other. He lathered my skull with shaving cream and gently ran the blade from back to front.

"Please just take me to bed. Please?" I begged, gazing up at him.

"Be patient," he whispered as he carefully removed what was left of my hair and gently ran his hand along my skull to make sure the stubble was gone.

I was glad he was there. I needed someone to think I was attractive. I wanted someone to pamper me, and yet I was unwilling to truly relinquish myself to him. I didn't want to be vulnerable. I didn't want to be totally honest. If I told him I was angry that he was dating other people, maybe he wouldn't come back. If I told him it pissed me off that he was always late, then maybe he would be mad at me. If I told him I was scared, maybe he would think I was weak. No. I would save face and let him shave my head, spend an hour or two in bed, and then wonder why I felt so empty when he left.

Someday, I hoped I would figure it all out. Someday.

Thursday, April 23, 2009

One of my sorority sisters, Sammy, and her five-year old daughter Campbell, came to visit from Seattle. We'd known each other for twenty-four years. Sammy was part of my college family—the one we'd created so long ago, back when we'd all been young and hopeful and just starting out on each of our life's adventures.

I opened the front door to greet my visitors. Her smiling blue eyes met mine.

"A scarf?" she laughed. "Are you kidding me? I want to see the real bald head!"

We tore the scarf off to reveal bald, bald, bald. We hugged. We cried. We laughed. All in thirty seconds.

"Who is this?" I asked about her little sidekick. The beautiful, bright child smiled at me as introductions were made, and she let me scoop her up into a big, warm hug. Cam was five years old and didn't seem scared to be around me.

"Come in. Come in. Throw your stuff wherever. Make yourself at home." It was extended family coming home, and I immediately felt warm and comfortable even though it had been years since we had been together. We did the quick tour of the house, had a quick snack, and assumed the position in front of the TV. Probably not great etiquette, but the TV and the sofa were really good coping mechanisms and made up my safety spot. Within a short time, we headed to bed, looking forward to spending the next day together. Punky and Mazey snuggled in next to me, and I closed my eyes and knew that this was what peace felt like.

Friends. Love. Cats. Simple.

Over morning coffee, we reminisced about college and her life over the past twenty years: her trips to Israel and Africa, her family and friends in Seattle. She talked enthusiastically about Cam and her younger daughter Sage. My friend had been busy, and had lived a life full of adventure and travel. She'd become a loving, caring mother and a devoted wife. I felt a twinge of insecurity as I opened a can of cat food for my chubby feline family.

Our day was spent visiting our alma mater—checking out the dorms, the houses, the bars, and the pizza joints.

"My favorite Mexican restaurant in the whole wide world is El Loco. On Lark Street. Can we go?"

"Whatever you want, my friend," I replied. "Mexican it is."

We scooted into the wooden booths and ordered a chimichanga and burritos. Campbell was happy with nachos and salsa as Sammy told her daughter about some of her G-rated escapades from days gone by. The fair-haired child with perfect freckles went on coloring on the designated placemat as we revisited the late eighties and chewed on some spicy substance. Eventually, the herpes in my mouth started to react to the hot sauce and my tongue started to swell. I didn't want to cut our visit short, though, so I didn't want to say anything. But my mouth kept getting smaller, and I couldn't concentrate on our conversation. Tears started to drip from my eyes.

"My tongue is swelling. I have herpes. I'm so sorry. I really want you guys to enjoy your time here."

Sam's look was one of total empathy and compassion. "Oh, lovey. It's okay. We just want to be with you. No matter where." She asked for the check and we quickly headed out the front door and into the car. It was hard for me to talk, so Sammy and Cam carried the conversation on about their world and their interests and I got a better snapshot into the life of my friend as we headed home.

I wasn't really used to having a five-year-old stay at the house with me, and felt a bit uncertain as to how to entertain her other than just plopping her in front of the TV. Sam was a great mother and encouraged her daughter to explore and wander as we sipped our tea in the living room. Before long, we heard a click, click, click noise coming down the hallway. As Campbell made her way into the living room, I stared in joyous wonder at the clever, three-foot creature standing in front of me. Her devilish smile made me howl in appreciation of her outfit—she had obviously found my closet. Her tiny feet were swimming in three-inch-high red pumps. A sparkly blue scarf was wrapped around her neck. Her head was covered in a long, bleached blonde wig complete with bangs. She strutted to the middle of the room and posed with the style of a runway model, hands bolted to her hips and her head tilted just so.

"Wait. Wait right there. I have to get a picture of this," I giggled as I ran to the family room in search of my camera.

"Show me again," I smiled as I snapped one picture after another.

"Wait, wait. Let me get pictures of the two of you together," Sammy offered.

I cuddled in next to my newest playmate. It was a photo shoot in the making. Campbell tried on the red wig and the purple scarf. I wore the blonde wig and green sunglasses. We posed for the camera. *Click. Click. Click.*

"How do you spell fun?" I asked Campbell.

She smiled at me as she sounded out the letters. "F-U-N."

"Yes, F-U-N. Fun!" I yelled with glee.

Campbell changed into the brunette pixie-cut and orange shawl as I grabbed the black baseball cap with the fake hair attached. Click. Click. Click. For an hour, we played dress-up and laughed and joked and posed. Yes, the baldness bugged me, but what else could I possibly do other than embrace it and look at it through the eyes of a five-year-old?

Friday, April 24, 2009

This morning was another plastic surgery, boob blow up visit. I was working on being positive about the fact that someday I would be through with this process. Someday things would be different. Someday things would change. And with that came some revelations.

I am going to die. Yes. I Am. There is no way out of this life alive. It's pretty basic. I will die. That basic knowledge allows me to do everything else that I want to with a feeling of purpose. It allows me to live my life. Add to this my belief that there is a BIG GUY up there driving the ship. Since I am not Him, I don't know when, where, or how I am going to die. And… that's brilliant! It's beautiful! I've heard all those hokey, corny, trite sayings before: *Each day is a gift. Each day is a blessing. Each day is something new that we get to do. It's a surprise, like a twenty-four-hour party, day after day.*

Before this point, I'd typically viewed these sayings as cute little hand-painted wooden signs that people hung in their kitchens or living rooms. But now the words seemed to take on new meaning.

It was so easy to take things for granted—small things, big things, whatever—but I had come to a point where I didn't want to anymore. I wanted to say what I needed to say in the moment. I wanted to be authentic and real. I wanted to be true to myself. There was only so much time in this life. Why should I fake it?

Thank you, cancer, for this gift of reality.

I hoped I could carry it with me.

Monday, April 27, 2009

My cousin Shannon was home from St. John, and we met in Woodstock, Vermont for a little weekend getaway. The Woodstock Inn combined elegance and rustic decor in a relaxed and natural setting. My baldness consumed my thoughts as we made our way to the receptionist. The black and tan paisley scarf on my head was the only article of clothing I wore that was remotely interesting—big, black fat pants and a black sweater had become my standard attire.

I found comfort in wearing loose, baggy clothes nowadays. A potato sack would have been my favorite outfit if it had come in something other than burlap. Mirrors were a thing of the past for me. I hated them. My eyebrows and eyelashes had disappeared. I'd tried the stick-on lashes—no good. I'd tried to draw in eyebrows—disaster.

I was becoming more and more naked. I felt vulnerable and uncomfortable and exposed.

In a twisted, sick sort of way, I was fortunate Shannon had been around cancer for most of her adult life—first her sister and then her mother had both been victims of the disease. She really didn't have much tolerance for my pity parties.

"You're fine," she kept repeating as we checked in and made our way to the lavish room. Immediately, we tossed our bags on the floor and collapsed onto our beds. I took off the scarf and rolled onto my side. Shannon was staring at me. She hadn't seen me bald yet.

"You look beautiful!" She grinned.

I felt my cheeks flush, and replied, "Really? I feel like a leper. How come there are no other bald people around? If so many people have cancer, why am I the only bald one around? Why is it so hidden?"

Being in the same room as her allowed me to be real. She got it. She understood. We talked about her mom and her sister and about what chemo had been like for them. How long the treatments were. How long they stayed in remission. How long before it came back and how long before they died. We talked about what it was like for her, about how she would take them to all the doctor appointments, how she would make her mother go for walks, and how she was so sad that I was going through this.

The next morning, I felt a hand shaking my arm.

"Get up! We're going for a walk," Shannon said.

Sleepily, I glanced over at the clock. *Six a.m.*

I rolled my eyes, knowing my "I have cancer" card wouldn't work with her. She knew I needed the exercise.

I pulled my larger-than-normal fanny out of the extra comfy bed, got dressed, and followed her outside. I concentrated on putting one foot in front of the other for a really slow three miles down the scenic Vermont roads. The sun was shining, the sky was an amazing hue of blue filled with white puffy clouds, the green grass was springing up, buds were on the trees, and tulips were bursting to bloom. The air had a feeling of lightness to it. *Spring. Rebirth. Rejuvenation.*

How do we put words to our heart? How do conversations about living happen from the soul? The idea of each moment being precious is exhausting and can only be talked about for so long. The deep shit had to turn into *"What should we have for lunch?" "Do you love being in the islands?" "What is your family up to?"*

Shannon didn't have children, either. We had a special bond because of this. Our siblings had little people to focus on. Our lives had taken us on different paths, and so it was especially important for me to spend time with her. She understood this dynamic of being child-less in a way that other people didn't. God, why did it seem like everything was soo big and soo deep? It was so much easier just watching TV.

We found little shops to wander through even though neither of us really wanted to spend money. We found a place to have a peaceful, non- herpes-stimulating meal. I needed a nap after that, and as we dropped into our beds, I farted out loud. It was loud and juicy and disgusting, and we laughed so hard that we cried. Thank God. Thank God. Thank God.

When I returned home from my weekend escape from reality, cars lined my driveway. *What's going on?* I grabbed my luggage and went into the house.

Through my kitchen window, I saw what I like to call "Love in Motion." A group of my girlfriends had infested my backyard. Pile after pile of leaves made their way to the front of the house. My yard was filled with countless women with rakes and tarps, all laughing together as they cleaned. I smiled and hugged each of them, my heart bursting with gratitude.

The sunlight was warm on my face as I sat on the deck with this dirty, messy, sweaty bunch of women, admiring a clean backyard. They smiled and talked about their plans for the afternoon. I nodded and looked into the eyes of these kind and loving women, the whole time holding back my tears. How could I ever repay their kindness?

Saturday, May 2, 2009

When my fortieth birthday started to creep up on me, my biological clock started ticking loudly. Driving past softball games or watching kids eat ice cream made me weep. Attending family-oriented parties became a test of strength. I had imagined being part of a family, being pregnant, feeling a baby's heartbeat inside me, hearing the coos of a little one, and the smelling baby powder in a little blue room. That was two years ago.

Now that option is gone. Everything is gone. Chemo put me into early menopause. Night sweats, no period, hot flashes, mood swings.

Thank you, cancer. Thank you, chemo. You both suck.

As I pulled the covers up around my neck, wiggled my toes, and let my cats purr in my ear, I had to let go of the idea that a baby would bring me closer to one of those "perfect" lives. I also had to let go of the idea that there was a "perfect" man out there to make my life better.

The only one responsible for my life was me.

Shit.

Sunday, May 3, 2009

I thanked the Big Guy every day that Aimee was living with me.

As soon as my eyes fluttered opened, I was flooded with emotions and panic. The mere act of getting out of bed seemed beyond my capabilities.

"How you doing?" Aimee asked as I schlepped down the hallway to the kitchen table.

She had no idea that my brain was a loaded cannon ready to explode. She poured me a cup of coffee as my body started to convulse with sobs. I buried my head in my hands. Aimee sat at the table with me, rubbing my head, waiting for the rest of my rant.

"I don't know how I am and I don't know what would make me better. I don't know what I want. Where do I want to live? I have to leave the house for track season. I need to find someplace to go for six weeks. Do I want to work? Who am I? Who do I want to be? I've been a bitch my whole life: being nasty to my husband, having one affair after another, using people, being self-centered to the extreme, and manipulating and maneuvering to get my way. My life has hinged on money and my ego and my need for attention. I have blamed everyone else for all the bad decisions in my life. I don't want to be like that anymore. I don't."

She handed me tissues by the fist-full and I wiped my face and threw them to the ground, creating a growing pile of snot-filled paper.

She nodded her head and said, "Yeah, I've been there, too. I've felt lower than whale shit. I've felt that way. You're not alone."

Whale Shit. Wow. I'd never heard that expression before.

I gasped for air and raised my eyes to look at her.

"I'm so glad we're friends," she said, smiling her dazzling smile. Her arms wrapped around me and I collapsed into her warmth.

Thanks, Big Guy, for sending Aimee my way.

Sunday, May 10, 2009, Mother's Day

I was such an asshole. I had some crazy old behaviors that, no matter how hard I tried to shake them, they just wouldn't go away. I was becoming a raging stalker on Facebook. I kept checking—obsessively checking—Crack's profile, trying to figure out who he'd been with recently, what he hadn't been telling me, and what was going on in his life. I was relentless, spinning fantasy stories in my head and making the worst of the situation.

What the hell was I thinking? Hadn't years of therapy fixed me at all? Wasn't I supposed to be more evolved? Wasn't I supposed to be aware of how much pain I was inflicting on myself?

The normal thought pattern of "Pick up the phone and have a conversation with him" never occurred to me. It was beyond my capabilities.

I was a pretty productive salesperson who probably appeared to be relatively put together from the outside. What people didn't see was the chaos, drama, and whirlwind energy playing ping pong inside my soul. Being around Crack did this to me. He was my drug. It was like taking a bong hit and then doing stupid shit.

And, to top it all off, it was Mother's Day. I was going through menopause and chemo and I wouldn't have kids and I had married someone twenty-five years older than me—and somehow my brain told me that none of it was a big deal. My thought process told me to just ignore it, push on through it, and carry on.

Guess what? My thought process was wrong. All that shit was a big deal.

I literally stayed in bed the whole day. Praying. Crying. Asking the Big Guy for guidance. What did He want me to do?

Cats. Covers. Tired. Weeping. Sleeping.

Mother's Day was always challenging, but this one was epic. There was no way around it. Just through it.

Monday, May 11, 2009

"Want to rub my head?" I asked a little guy in the elevator at the department store. He looked like he had just seen his first alien. He was probably surprised that alien women could actually talk, but he did a good job of not crying as he shrank against his mother's leg and held on for dear life.

"You look so beautiful," the mother replied as she gently placed her hand on her son's shoulder. She had a full head of brown curly locks.

I bent over and offered my head to the kid, just in case he was curious and wanted to feel it. But he simply moved closer to his mom, his eyes wide. I smiled and stood up.

I guess he didn't want to touch an alien.

I had recently started to notice how different my physical features appeared. No hair led to bigger eyes and whiter teeth. After Crack shaved the stubble off my head, an obvious line of demarcation emerged like a halo around my head. The part of my head that used to be home to a thick head of blonde hair was now snow white while the rest of my face had color from the sun. I resorted to using the self-tanning, foaming stuff to minimize the seemingly stark line.

Some strangers actually had the courage to ask me, "Are you sick?"

My answer was always the same: "Thank you so much for asking. Thanks for being so open about it. Yes. I have cancer."

I often went out in public bald. I didn't want to hide this disease. I wanted to create an awareness. If so many people had cancer, why weren't there more bald chicks running around? People would try to avoid the subject of my baldness, seeking any opportunity to pretend that I wasn't bald. They squirmed and fidgeted and fixed their eyes directly on mine, trying to steer clear of the elephant in the middle of the room. I wouldn't let them off the hook and instead I initiated the conversation about cancer. I wouldn't let people ignore this, no matter how uncomfortable it was for them. I was angry and aggressive. This was real. This was what cancer looked like. *Welcome to my world. Denial be smashed. Mine and yours.*

Tuesday, May 12, 2009

Aimee had become the queen of quiche. Cheese quiche. Spinach quiche. Broccoli quiche. Quiche and eggs with toast. These were the things that helped my belly after chemo, along with personal microwaveable pizzas and potatoes.

On chemo days, my stomach screamed for steak because of the steroids. I ate what felt good. I constantly read about organic living, fruits and vegetables, and anti-oxidants that were supposed to fight cancer, but I didn't care. I couldn't do it. Carrots didn't cut it for me. Chemo made me feel like shit. If my stomach said mint chocolate chip ice cream was what it wanted, then that was what it got.

The down side? I had to buy bigger pants. My chemo belly was getting all those tight pant marks around the waist and I was having a hard time bending over to pick things up. I really had hoped that I would lose a few pounds with this cancer and chemo thing. It wasn't working out like I had planned.

Sunday, May 17, 2009

Marie and I spent the afternoon in the pool at the YMCA. I didn't need to wear a swim cap, but I did realize that I needed to order a new bathing suit with patterns because the stupid expanders in my chest were all screwy—*and* not symmetrical *and* oddly shaped. The scar marks screamed for attention through the solid red Speedo suit.

I paddled my way up and down the pool one lap at a time. I had to stop and rest regularly, though—a side effect of having not worked out much these last few months. Another lap. Breathe. I felt a pull in my chest and wondered if I would sink because of these fake boobs that were attached to my chest that felt like bricks.

At each break, Marie and I talked about how to improve our stroke, or rather, how not to drown. We stretched our bodies some more, kicking from the hips and keeping our heads down. Arm over arm. Breath after breath. We practiced and played around in the pool like eight-year-olds and then hung out in the sauna chatting about furniture and the post office and what to cook for dinner.

Wednesday, May 27, 2009

Yesterday was chemo number six. Six down. Two to go. My final chemo treatment was scheduled for June 23rd.

I spent most of the afternoon picking weeds out of my flowerbed. As I pulled random growth from the middle of the peonies and the lilies, a wave of sadness came over me. Last year, I'd pulled weeds in an effort to revive myself from my recent marital separation. Twelve months later, my flowerbed had become my haven for my cancer treatments. I was keenly aware of the difference a year makes.

Over the last three-hundred-and-sixty-five days, I had been given the gift of desperation. I had been forced to grow up. I had been relieved of my need to please other people. I could talk about nipple removal, scars across my chest, and how bald was beautiful. I could talk about death and dying and mortality, and yet I had still not gotten the hang of having an adult conversation with someone I was sleeping with.

As I looked at the year in retrospect, it became apparent that I had experienced a lot of growth because of this cancer thing. It was also clear that there was still work to do. A deep, unsettling fear started to formulate and rear its ugly head. What about after going through all this treatment—the surgery, chemo, radiation—what about if there was still cancer in my bones or one little loose cancer cell floating around someplace? No matter how hard I tried to not think about recurrence, the possibility existed. And the reality shown within my family history was that people got cancer, doctors treated it, it went into remission, and then it came back and people died. THAT was my reality. And it smacked me square in the face as I got closer to finishing chemo.

Did I do everything? Everything possible? What about those antioxidants I didn't eat, or all the carbs I put in my system? I wasn't perfect, but I supposed I'd given it my best shot. I didn't have any control over this. I never had and I never would.

I had to practice learning to let it go.

Tuesday, June 23, 2009

Today was my last day of chemo. I left the hospital, delivered a sample chair, and headed back to the world of "normal". Or so I wanted to believe.

Friday, July 3, 2009

Work was the same as usual; moving tables and chairs, updating literature, doing quotes, and then dealing with phone calls, phone calls, and more phone calls. Emails, emails, and more emails. Everything was the same as when I'd started the cancer journey. Nothing had changed. Except me.

Sunday, July 5, 2009

My buddy Jackie invited me to Lake Placid for Fourth of July weekend. Lake Placid. Serene. Peaceful. A favorite spot of mine.

I spent the two-hour drive up the Northway and then along twisty Route 73 pondering the next part of my life. What happened now?

If I could do anything and live anywhere, what would my life look like? I had imagined buying a house and what that would feel like. *Claustrophobic* was the word that came to mind.

There was something telling me to dream. Just dream big. I imagined different places I could go: Montana, St. John, Spain. I wondered about jobs and careers and asked myself what I liked: people, creativity, problem solving, writing, traveling, painting pictures with words, exercising, laughing. I couldn't think of a job where I could get paid to do all this.

My first job was picking tomatoes in a field with a bunch of Jamaicans at the age of fourteen. I would hop on the back of Dad's motorcycle and he would drop me off at the field on his way to work. Starting time was six thirty a.m. I remember the sweet pungent odor of insecticides filling the air when it got hot. Bubba, a large, tall Jamaican man, worked next to me. Sometimes his accent was so thick that it was difficult to decipher what he said. I plucked tomato after tomato off the vines and gently placed each one into little round woven baskets. I did this over and over again, up and down the rows, all day long, the sun beating down on my back. The bright fruits were later rinsed, shined, and staged in new baskets for presentation. A hard day's worth of work was what was expected of us, and I am so grateful to have learned the lesson. That first job served me well. It taught me a strong work ethic, the value of a dollar, and humility. No matter what my career did or the down-turn in the economy or the desperation felt by those around me, I knew that I could always pick tomatoes if I needed to. The downside? To this day, I can't eat those little red squishy vegetables.

Typically, I spent Fourth of July with my family eating strawberry shortcake, hot dogs, hamburgers, and potato chips. But this one was different. Jackie's dad was an equine vet, and there was a big dressage event going on in town. It was also forty-two degrees. Fahrenheit. We wandered around the stables and the riding arenas and the vendor booths as I pulled my jacket closer. Horse people traipsed around in those skin-tight black riding pants, high leather boots, and fancy helmets. Majestic animals pranced proudly down walkways as if to show off their shiny coats. A slight mist turned into small ice pellets that were beating on my tender bald head. *Can't we just have a hot dog someplace? And doesn't anyone sell winter hats here?* I was out of my element. These were pretty wealthy people, and some pretty famous people's names were getting thrown around. I just wanted to buy a scarf to cover my head so all the heat wouldn't disappear and I wouldn't die of hyperthermia.

We found a cute little vendor shop and wrapped a small blanket around my skull. I tried to look elegant and rich and fashionable, but somehow the mini-blanket just didn't make the grade.

We visited Jackie's dad, petted a few horses, and did another loop around the fairgrounds before heading back to the house. There, we started a small fire inside the lovely

Adirondack cottage that was nestled in the pine trees. The living room windows opened onto the lake, and we watched the heavy rain/sleet fall outside, chatting about horses and jobs and kids and how it really wasn't supposed to be this cold on the Fourth of July. As night fell, we wrapped sleeping bags around our shoulders and sat on the dock, watching fireworks explode over the water and hoping not to get frostbite. My friend was entertaining me. She was helping me pass the time. She had become my extended family and I loved her.

Lake Placid was a great place, even when it snowed in the middle of the summer. Just as long as you had the right company.

Monday, July 6, 2009

Let the radiation begin.

Instead of using black sharpies to mark my body up, the radiation oncologist upgraded me to tattoos. Four little dots were strategically placed on my chest. These were the points that the laser light beams/radiation equipment would use for consistency. Five days a week for six weeks, I would go to the hospital, change into one of those flimsy little gowns, march myself into the lead-walled room, lay on a cold table, and let technicians line my tattoos up with red laser lines that were coming out of the ceiling and the walls.

The radiation oncologist, Dr. Foster, had prepared me for the side effects.

"One of the side effects is fatigue. Some people get it. Others don't. You won't know until you are into the process."

I nodded my head. Yeah, I knew about fatigue. I was opting out of this version of it.

"The radiation will also burn your skin. By the end of your treatment, you will probably have a square mark on your chest. Most likely, there will also be an exit burn on your back where the rays go through your body. We will position the beams so as to not hit your lungs, but you could also have some difficulty breathing. We'll want to keep an eye on these things."

I was like a bobble-head doll. "Okay, Doc. Whatever you say."

Aimee was seated at the kitchen table when I got home.

"You're never going to believe this," I snapped as I opened the freezer door and took out the ice cream.

She was so used to my mood swings by this point that she very calmly looked up from the paper and asked, "What's up?"

"I have to go in for radiation for five days a week for six weeks. And I'm going to end up with a big-ass red burnt square on my chest. It's getting to be tank-top weather. It's going to look like shit. A red square burn mark under a sexy, cute tank top. I've got these new boobs and don't have to wear a bra and it is STILL going to look like shit!" I exclaimed, shoving a spoonful of mint chocolate chip into my mouth. I took a breath following my rant and stared at my friend, full of contempt and anger.

Aimee looked at me with a wide smirk on her face. "So... I guess you've gotten used to being bald."

Monday, July 13, 2009

Today was supposed to be my first radiation treatment. I arrived early with the assumption that it would be a breeze like everyone said, only to find a waiting room full of people and some of my competitor's furniture. I had conveniently left my phone at home—thinking this was going to take fifteen minutes—so I took up residence in the lobby with the paper and an easy Sudoku puzzle.

The waiting area reminded me of a coffee shop. There was a self-help coffee machine with all the fixings to go with it. The newspapers were neatly placed on the coffee tables and everyone was chatting away with each other. I felt like the new kid on the block. I didn't really want to be part of this makeshift support group, though. *Couldn't we just get on with it and be done?* I wanted to get in, get zapped, and get back on the road to selling chairs. I plugged my ear buds into my head and turned on my iPod.

Then Jessica, one of the nurses, stood up in the middle of the waiting room and shouted, "We hate to do this to you, but the radiation equipment is having technical difficulties! Repairmen are in route. The machine will be back up tomorrow."

I was suddenly reminded of a magnet on my refrigerator that said, "We Plan. God Laughs." Perfect.

Friday, July 17, 2009

Spike was out of Afghanistan. I received an email that said he no longer needed to wear vests or weapons and that he was working on getting to Germany and then to BWI. For the first time in a long time, I felt some relief. He was making his way to the States. He was out. He was safe.

Radiation treatment started today, and it was easy.

Sunday, July 19, 2009

Track season was quickly approaching. Walls had been washed down and repainted. Winter clothes were relocated to the basement closets. Summer clothes were shoved in tubs and stacked in the back of the mini-van. Towels and sheets were neatly folded and stacked in the linen closet. Kitchen cabinets were emptied, wiped down, and restacked. The owner's artwork was re-hung on the walls. My parents had picked up Mazey and Punky, and would keep them at kitty camp for the summer. Aimee and I were moving out the following weekend, going our separate ways.

I was headed to the spare room in Marie's house for the next five weeks, and Aimee was headed elsewhere for the next phase of her life. I was going to miss her. I was going to miss her humor, her candor, and her quiche. She had become my sister, my nurse, and my therapist. The house would be lonely when I returned in September without her.

Crack was talking to me more than usual. I visualized what any future with him would be like; insanity, chaos, and drama. I had to listen (and actually hear him) when he told me that the mortgage company was calling him on a regular basis. I had to listen when he told me that his house was disgusting and in disarray. I had to listen when he said that he couldn't commit to people. I had to listen to him rant that he had a hard time talking to men and that he had women friends all over the place.

But the more I listened to him, the more I realized that I didn't want to live like that. I didn't want to be chasing him, trying to change him, and forcing things to be the way that I wanted them to be. I needed to just let go. I needed to let go every time I thought of him. I needed to stop thinking about him. It was easier said than done. This shitty feeling I was having about myself was getting old.

While I was trying to actually hear every single word Crack said to me, I conveniently decided to ignore Dr. Foster's warnings about fatigue. I imagined I could somehow magically escape this side effect.

During one of my early trips to the radiation center, I actually unplugged from my iPod and struck up a conversation with another patient named Jennifer. She looked to be a bit younger than me, with beaming blue eyes that matched the scarf wrapped around her head. After the obligatory pleasantries, I got to the point.

"How long have you been doing this?" I asked, not sure I wanted to know the answer.

"I've been around for four weeks. I'm almost done." Her smile made her face glow.

"Are you tired? The doctor said some people get tired and some don't. Are you tired?" I was relentless in my quest to know if I would spend more time in bed.

"Nope. I'm not tired. It's been pretty easy."

I sank deeper into the teal green lounge chair and let out a sigh of relief. She said she wasn't tired. There was hope.

He was wrong. I knew he was wrong. *I will not get tired. I will not get tired. I will not get tired.*

I needed to keep a positive outlook and surround myself with people who would coach me and remind me that I wasn't in charge. I needed to let go of the things I couldn't control. The Big Guy was taking care of me and I was learning lessons. I was going to let him direct me.

Monday, July 20, 2009

4:30 a.m. My eyes snapped open. I was headed to a spin class. I saw the sun rise. I felt the morning air. I felt that "high" from being up early.

I entered the dimly lit spin room. Music hummed in the background as cyclists adjusted their seat height, handlebars, and loaded their water bottles. My bald head and fat ass made their way onto a bike. Good looking, hard-body instructor Gene climbed onto the bike located at the head of the room. His enthusiasm set the tone. High-energy music reverberated through my body as my legs pushed and pulled the pedals. I climbed hills and raced down the other side. Sweat poured out of my bald head. Air went in and out of my lungs. Time stood still as I felt every muscle in my body activate. I was alive!

Next stop? Radiation Oncology Center. It was Monday, and I needed to meet with the doctor for my weekly check-up. I sat in the exam room wearing yet another flimsy gown and answering emails until I heard a slight knock on the door. A different guy walked in and shook my hand.

"Hi, Bethany. I'm Dr. Heller. Dr. Foster is on rounds today, so I'll be doing your exam. Okay?"

As if there was an option?

I shook his hand and smiled politely, unphased by the fact that I was half-dressed.

"Nice to meet you."

"How's it going? How do you feel today?" he asked as he pulled up the small black vinyl stool opposite me.

"Great!" My response was full of adrenaline. "I did a spin class this morning."

His gaze abruptly shifted from the manila folder to my face. His big brown eyes looked as if they were about to pop out of his head.

"What's the matter?" I asked, suddenly worried. "Am I restricted from doing that stuff?"

"Maybe you could do some less intense activities. After chemo, your energy tank was only half-full. Radiation is going to zap what's left of it. You won't bounce back like you usually would."

I didn't like this guy.

"During the first two weeks of radiation, you might not notice a big difference. By weeks three, four, and five, your energy will dwindle. By week six, you'll want out of this program in a big way."

He obviously didn't understand. I wanted out now! Why did he have to tell me that? He didn't know me. I was opting for the non-fatigue version of this program. The other doctor, Dr. Foster, had said it was a fifty-fifty chance; a fifty percent chance I would get tired, a fifty percent chance I wouldn't.

I was determined to not get tired. I wouldn't get tired!

Wednesday, July 29, 2009

I didn't like being wrong. I didn't like it one bit, but I finally had to succumb to the idea that maybe Dr. Heller knew more than me about radiation and fatigue.

Exhaustion started to kick in today. Though angry and resentful, I finally let go yet again. I shut off my phone and climbed into bed.

Tuesday, August 4, 2009

As I pulled into my parents' driveway, my monster of a brother came running out to greet me. I bolted from the minivan and rushed into Spike's arms. I also flinched in pain as he embraced me with a bear hug. I had completely forgotten about the expanders in my chest.

"Jesus," Spike laughed as he looked at my chest. "What are those things poking me?"

"Oh! My bricks, you mean?" I snickered. "Yeah. That's my life lately. Bricks and baldness. I love you, too."

I loved my family. No bullshit. No hidden agendas. Everything was right out there on the table.

We passed the weekend doing the same things we had done for forty years: playing cards with Mom, taking rides with Dad, pizza dinner, reviews of the most current *People* magazines, trips to the mall, and the normal sarcasm and lack of sympathy.

Sunday morning, Spike and I got up early to go to Dunkin Donuts together. I needed some one-on-one time with this warrior. I needed to check in with his true spirit.

Over coffee and donuts, he told me stories of dirt roads, the Taliban, al-Qaeda, and Osama bin Laden. He shared stories about IEDs, young soldiers traumatized by war, and loving families living in lands far away. His experiences were a portal into the bigger picture—the bigger picture of the world beyond me and beyond cancer.

Unfortunately, the weekend passed too quickly, and within the blink of an eye, it was Monday morning and I was back at the radiation center again. The stupid doctor who'd told me I was going to be tired walked into the exam room. My flimsy gown drooped around my slumped shoulders as he asked how I felt. Tears flowed freely as another form of surrender hit my soul.

"I don't want to be tired anymore. I don't want to do this anymore. I want to stop. I am so mad that you were right."

The mascara from my eleven eyelashes was smudged around my eyes. Dr. Heller handed me a box of tissues.

I blew my nose, sniffled some, and cleared my throat, trying to grab onto any little piece of dignity that was available to me.

"I'm so mad. So mad. And sad."

He nodded quietly as I perched myself on the exam table. The flimsy gown was pushed aside so he could scrutinize my left breast, the one covered with a red square of a burn mark.

"It looks good. Everything is happening just like it should. You are more than halfway there. Be gentle with yourself. Be patient. Go home and rest."

I nodded and wiped the residue from my face as we trudged down the hallway. I gave a weepy nod to the nurses and the technicians as I found my position on the cold metal table in the lead room. Red laser beams aligned with my tattoo freckles. Slight buzzing noises filled the room.

We were killing cancer cells. Or at least that was the plan.

Ten minutes later, I removed my body from the metal table and headed to the dressing room. I dropped the flimsy gown and stood bare-chested in the square room staring at the pretty blue and brown pillows on the bench. I gently applied moisturizer to my breast/brick/chest and slipped into my loose-fitting patterned blouse. I sniffled and said good-bye to the nurses.

"See you tomorrow." I was resigned to continuing to process.

I headed out the door, climbed into my minivan, and got on with my day; chairs, tables, emails, anything to distract me from my current life situation. By four o'clock, the doctor's words actually resonated in my brain.

Okay. Okay. I give up! I will rest!

I climbed into bed yet again, pulled the covers over my battered body, cuddled with my cats, and released myself from the torture of yet another day. It was getting old. It was kind of bullshit. It was fucking annoying. Yet, it was the way it had to be.

Monday, August 10, 2009

The rest of the week—Tuesday through Friday—was better than Monday. I showed up at the hospital every day, got zapped, rested, and then repeated the whole process over again the next day. Before I knew it, it was Meltdown Monday again.

It started off like most Mondays, me sitting in the exam room with my Blackberry and waiting for someone to poke at my chest. Dr. Foster—the doctor I liked—entered the room. I was happy to see him.

"I've got good news."

Already, this was a great way to start the day.

"You're going to be released a week early."

My mind barely had enough time to process his words before I burst into tears.

"A week early?" I muttered, my lips quivering with joy as tears flowed freely down my cheek. "Are you sure? Am I okay? I'll do another week if it means that I won't have any cancer cells running around. Really, I will. Are you sure?"

Dr. Foster calmly rattled on about numbers and statistics related to radiation.

"We tell patients to plan on six weeks. If they respond well to the treatment, we let them out early. It would be tough to tell someone to expect five weeks and then tell them they needed to do more. That's not easy to comprehend."

My head bounced up and down, totally understanding why things were presented the way they were. *No way.* There was no way I would have handled it well if they'd told me I needed to do more than planned. You might as well have checked me into the mental health unit. I got it.

I was getting released early. Things were looking good. I cried anyway. I couldn't stop smiling. It felt like Christmas.

Friday, August 14, 2009

My brain shifted gears into production and real-life mode. Things needed to be taken care of. I needed to get a legal separation. I needed to make a decision about how to live. Should I buy a house, travel around the world, live near my family? How could I possibly deal with all the people in my life? How was I supposed to manage my time? I wanted to create some stability. I was trying to get back on the *Peace and Serenity* wagon.

During one of my last visits with Crack, we sat at my kitchen table and ate peanut butter and jelly sandwiches. I finally had the guts to ask those difficult questions.

"What do you want from me?"

He sat in silence with no answer. As I waited for his response, I asked myself the same thing. *What am I trying to get? Why did I even bother to see him again? What do I want?* The answers were easy for me.

I knew my motives: I wanted to feel attractive. I wanted someone to pay attention to me. I wanted to feel loved.

But Crack couldn't do that for me. It had never been about love with him. It had always been about lust. It was my selfish need for an adrenaline hit. And then it became about power and control. My desire to control him and to change him. My need for power over the situation and my wanting to make things work out the way that I wanted them to work out. I was not willing to accept the fact that he did not want to have a relationship with just me. I had pushed and shoved and chased and obsessed until I couldn't anymore.

When he left that day, an overwhelming sense of reality filled me. I was sure my life was meant for something more. *Don't be scared to be alone and trust that it will all work out. Breathe in. Breathe out. Breathe in. Breathe out.*

Later that week, I texted Crack. "Please do not contact me again."

I had finally come to the end of my rope and was fed up with my insanity. I was tired of the chaos and drama. The stupid game in my head had out-lived its usefulness. Amazingly, I had a lot of extra time on my hands when I wasn't obsessively checking my phone or Facebook or stalking him or his girlfriend or whoever else I thought was in his life. I no longer imagined what he was doing or where he was. I didn't sit waiting for him to show up. I no longer pretended that he cared. I was done.

There were moments of uncertainty, of course. Moments when I felt insecure and alone. Could I really let go of him that easily? Could I really just move on? Could I really allow for the potential of something else? Could I really be okay being single?

I had resigned myself to the possibility that maybe I could.

Thursday, August 20, 2009

As I was getting ready to retire from radiation, I realized I would miss the little coffee club that assembled in the hospital lobby every morning. I had begrudgingly become part of the makeshift support group and had enjoyed hearing the stories of other radiation patients.

For instance, Danielle had finished three weeks before. She was bald and wore a great scarf every day. She'd had breast cancer, surgery, chemo, and radiation. Her graduation present from radiation was a weekend trip to Ogunquit Beach in Maine with her husband and five-year-old son. She wasn't tired at all during radiation. *Why wasn't she tired? Why did she get to breeze through? It must be difficult going through treatment with a five-year-old.*

When Sally first arrived at the coffee club, she had long, blonde, beautiful hair. Months prior, she had been diagnosed with inoperable lung cancer. Her first set of treatments consisted of radiation and chemo. The treatments did not combat the aggressive disease. Cancer had spread to her brain. Every day when she went into the room with the lead walls, she was fitted up with a metal screen mask that would allow the red laser light beams to hit the exact point in her brain. Yesterday when she arrived, she was bald. Tomorrow is her last day of treatment. The doctors are not offering her many options.

Jim and his wife June became my friends during my last week of treatment. It was Jim's sixth time being treated for cancer over the last thirteen years. At eighty years old, he was handsome and elegant, always dressed in freshly-pressed khakis and a crisp white shirt. June was a petite, stunning woman with meticulous makeup and nails. Her jewelry was tasteful, which is another way to say really expensive. Jim's most recent tumor was on his throat and was inoperable. The goal of treatment was to shrink the mass and extend his life. He had lost his taste buds and had issues eating, which he said was one of his favorite pastimes. The couple trekked to the hospital twice a day for what they hoped would be a lifesaving treatment. *Lifesaving for how long?* I wondered.

Radiation Oncology waiting rooms are a tapestry of people, all with different stories.

Everyone in this one sat around chatting about their lives, their families, and their trials and tribulations. It was a complicated process. People came and went. Some went on to live their lives. Some died. And the world turned round and round, because that's how life is.

Saturday, August 22, 2009

During chemo, Saturdays were bed days. However, today I was ecstatic to pay bills, clean my car, and answer emails. I needed to prepare for my upcoming business trip on Monday. I was headed to Wisconsin for chair training. My whole body ached with exhaustion, but I was defiant. I had to work. I wanted to sell chairs again; I wanted to be productive and make money. I wanted to be back on the "real life" train.

Living in Marie's house was a new kind of adventure. Her kids, Cody and Dylan, were home for the summer. The family sat at the kitchen table and discussed student loans, summer jobs, dinner requests, getting apartments, and applications to med school, as well as what the social activities for the evening would be. The house was full of laughter and joking and intelligent conversation, with a few sarcastic digs thrown in on occasion just to keep everyone on their toes.

At night, I lay in the twin bed in the spare room and reviewed my day. My boob was burnt, sore, and getting blisters. It itched, and the stretch marks were hideous. I had ugly kumquat-shaped mounds on my chest. I looked like a freak. I wanted nipples again. I wanted to be able to feel my skin. I wanted the numbness to go away. I didn't want them to be bricks anymore. Sadly, no one had really asked me what I wanted. I just followed the doctors' orders.

Thursday, August 27, 2009

Over. Treatment was over.

My last day of radiation was Monday. I got a diploma, a gift, and skipped out of the hospital with a "thank you" and a smile that basically translated into: *"You guys are nice people but I hope I never, ever, ever see you again."*

I hopped in the minivan and made a beeline for the airport. It was imperative that I be in Wisconsin that afternoon. Some changes had happened with ownerships and corporate take-overs, and my job was mixed up in the transition. The economic downturn was upon us.

I was bald, burnt, and tired, but I sucked it up. I needed to be there. For the next two days, my peach fuzz head and I sat in a conference room in the basement of some high-end hotel learning as much as we could about chair construction details, computer transitions, and market share. All very important stuff.

Tuesday, September, 8, 2009

Track season in Saratoga had come to a close, which meant my time spent in the comfort of Marie's spare room was over. I packed up my two tubs of clothes and threw them in the back of the minivan. Mom and Dad met me at our standard drop-off point in Oneonta for the kitty exchange. Punky and Mazey smiled at me from the passenger seat as we made our way back to Saratoga. Within hours, we walked back into our home.

Aimee was gone. Crack was gone. Cancer was gone. The house was empty.

Tuesday, September 29, 2009

Most of the everyday cancer stuff was over. Translation: no more treatments and not too many doctor appointments. The emotional residue hangover was another story.

A week after radiation ended, an overwhelming sense of dread washed over me. There was suddenly no doubt in my mind that my cancer would come back and I would die. That's what had happened to my aunt and my cousin. Every cell in my body told me I was on borrowed time. It was knee-buckling and soul-crushing, and permeated every bit of awareness in my body. I was going to die. I sat on the sofa, watched TV, and cuddled with my cats for hours and hours and hours by myself. What else was there to do?

Thursday, October 8, 2009

Depression. Another side effect of cancer that no one talks about. Crying at the drop of a hat wasn't so peaceful. It also wasn't so great for the chair business. No doctor had warned me about this. The shame around not being able to get through one day without thinking about if I was really healthy and when I was going to die was debilitating. I hadn't been prepared to be bedridden because I didn't want to break down in a full blown sobbing session while talking about fabric selections.

I felt inadequate and ashamed.

Saturday, October 10, 2009

On Thursday, I met with my oncologist.

"Your tumor markers look good," said Dr. Miller.

"What does that mean?" I asked skeptically.

"It means that we've tested your liver enzymes and your body is functioning within normal parameters."

"So, are you telling me that there's a blood test that will predict whether or not my cancer is coming back?"

"We monitor the numbers and look for fluctuation in how your body is working."

"I don't believe you. I don't believe there's a blood test that can tell you if my cancer is back," I replied firmly. "It can't be. If this was true, why are there mammograms and ultrasounds and MRIs?"

I was defiant, belligerent, and in tears. I was a puddle dressed in a medical gown, sitting in a non-descript exam room with a doctor staring at me and trying to tell me I was alright.

"A common side effect of this process is depression," Dr. Miller explained with a blank stare. "I can prescribe something to help with this."

My shoulders heaved. My brain sank lower. I felt like I had been kicked in the stomach.

"Anti-depressants? You're kidding me, right? I'm the girl who handed out smiley-face buttons during chemo."

I felt ashamed and disappointed in myself. I'd assumed that all that therapy would have helped me get through this thing.

We made eye contact as I felt my life crumble just a little more.

"They will help. Just take them to stabilize your emotions. It's okay."

Couldn't he just give me more pain meds? Why did it have to be depression? It sounded so weak and needy. The pain meds took the edge off, too. *Whatever.* My brain followed his directions and we entered the anti-depression, mental health mode. *Gross.*

Later in the day, I called my brother. He reminded me about dirt roads and unfed children and car bombs and young soldiers wanting to commit suicide. He reminded me that everything was relative. Someone always had it worse.

These were the images I need to concentrate on when I was scared and angry and in bed sobbing. I had to remember gratitude, faith, and hope. There had to be some sort of brain switch to catch my thoughts and move them down another path. I had to become aware of options in my thinking.

Monday, November 2, 2009

My obsession with Crack had been lifted. I no longer had that need, that crazy compulsion to have him in my life. I had started feeling balanced and content, enjoying my cats and my life. I wasn't running. I wasn't chasing. I was simply relaxing and resting and letting life happen. It felt light and free and like something bordering on peace. Hmm. Coincidence that this happened after being on anti-depressants? What a novel idea.

Saturday, November 14, 2009

This week we installed furniture at the hospice unit at the local hospital. Mary was an eighty-year-old patient who was getting ready to leave the unit the following week. She was spry, functioning, alert, and extremely funny. The moment I met her, she touched my heart.

My job was to distract people so furniture installers could switch out the bedside cabinets, chairs, and recliners. Most of the people in the wing were sleeping and dying, but Mary was wide-awake and had lots of company.

"Hey, lady." She pointed at me from her bed. "What are you doing here?" She was aware of the commotion and curious.

"You're getting new furniture. Isn't that awesome? I'm here to make sure it goes okay. What are you doing here?" I asked her.

"Cancer. Breast cancer. But I'm getting ready to go home soon."

"You're going home? I didn't know people left this place while they were still alive." I hadn't meant to be rude, but it might have been.

She let out a huge belly laugh. "Yeah. Yeah. Well, I am going home. I'm not staying here that long. I want to be in my own house."

I could certainly understand that.

Mary had been diagnosed four years earlier. She'd had a mastectomy, and during the procedure one of her lungs had collapsed. Afterwards, she had infections and complications from surgery. She went through chemo and then aggressive radiation. She seemed pretty alert and energetic for going through what she had.

Mary had buried two husbands in her lifetime, but had not given up on love, and as she lay in her hospice bed, her main concern was that she might meet a man and that he wouldn't like her overly fuzzy beard and mustache. She was also pleased to announce that she had put on one of her nicer nightgowns that morning.

"You always gotta' look good. Just in case!" Her bright eyes smiled.

When the nurse entered the room and asked Mary about her pain level, a strong response of "seven" filled the room.

Whoa... I thought. *Seven?*

She was a symbol of grace and dignity, and didn't complain a bit.

As the movers replaced the cabinets and the seating, the chaplain came into the room. Mary and her family formed a circle to pray and I started to exit the room, allowing the family their privacy.

"Hey, lady!" Mary yelled. "Get back here."

I stopped at the door and turned around. I was invited into the circle. I smiled and joined hands with Mary and her family. The chaplain prayed for Mary's peace and one more day of life surrounded by love. Energy flowed through these strangers' hands into mine and the sense of contentment and belonging lasted for a full two minutes. Mary was a powerful example of spirit and acceptance. I hugged her, bid her farewell, and left the hospital in tears again.

Monday, November 23, 2009

It was the Monday before Thanksgiving again.

Julanne, Chey, Zach, and I were packed into the ever-dependable minivan. Mom and Dad were happy to be in their own vehicle ahead of us, complete with peace and quiet and no kids. The family was headed to see Spike and his girlfriend Tracy's house in St. Louis for Thanksgiving. Sixteen hours away. It was a caravan adventure.

The van was full of snacks, pillows, and blankets—just like when we'd been kids and we'd made the long journey to New Hampshire for every family holiday. The difference was that back then we hadn't had portable DVD players, iPods, or PlayStations. We'd had to play the picnic game or sing songs or fold paper into birds.

Everything else was pretty much the same. *"Don't touch me." "Mom, he's looking out my window." "Are we there yet?"* It felt very familiar and wonderful and nostalgic. It was during these moments—these precious, unforgettable moments—when I missed having kids.

As my niece and nephew slept in the back, my sister Julanne and I talked about the recent ultrasound on my ovaries. The tests had come back fine, but I was coming to terms with the fact that this cancer shit just wouldn't end. There would always be one more test, one more option, one more waiting period.

Since I was a young breast cancer survivor with no children, I was at a higher risk of developing ovarian cancer than most. Just one more issue to deal with. I wanted to stick my head in the sand and get on with my life. I just didn't want to hear anything else. I didn't want there to be any more problems. I didn't want to have another surgery.

My sister listened and then we crinkled our noses when a stench reached the front of the van.

"What did Zack eat yesterday? Oh my God. He must be rotten inside!" We howled as Julanne rolled down the windows and we made our way across Interstate 70.

Wednesday, November 25, 2009

My father, mother, sister, and niece and nephew and I sat in a medium-sized auditorium surrounded by men and women in fatigues. It was a quarterly awards ceremony for the members of the A2 division of the intelligence arm of the Air Force. The language they were speaking was foreign, full of acronyms and technical terms.

The commander was announced as she entered the room. Everyone rose and stood at attention. Straight backs. Straight arms. Heads high. They all held their hands a certain way. Closed fists with their thumbs tucked snuggly inside.

The quarterly meeting would start with the awards section. Spike, or Captain Donald W. Moss as he was known in the military, was called first. He walked to the stage at the front of the room and stood at attention next to his commander. Accolades were given for my brother's bravery during combat in Afghanistan. We were told that he had put his life in danger and that his actions had made a difference.

I remembered one of his phone calls back in June. He had called me during the week following an episode and had shared with me part of his experience. He'd talked about the Taliban and the IEDs and how they were NOT going to have their way with him, and certainly not the day after his birthday. He hadn't told our parents about this incident. He hadn't wanted them to worry. But his commander was now pinning a bronze star on my brother's chest. He was being recognized for an act of bravery during his active duty. I'm not sure if it was my brother's humble nature or the fact that some of what he does is super-duper top-secret Air Force stuff (or so I like to think), but the details of the incident were never discussed.

I sat in the seat next to my sister, tears filling both our eyes. My brother had witnessed war. He had done battle. He had seen things that no one should have to see. He had lived in a life-threatening situation for a year and now he was home, on stage, being commended for his bravery. The room was full of heroes, too—not just my brother. These men and women were doing something to protect our country every day that they went to work.

As I listened to the awards continue, I tried not to sob too loudly. I diverted my attention to the chairs and how they were bolted into the floor. The fabric didn't look familiar and the lectern wasn't from one of the factories I recognized. Following the ceremony, I would chat with my brother's girlfriend. She worked for the Air Force as well and maybe she could introduce me to someone in the procurement office of one our local Air National Guard offices. Maybe I could talk to them about furniture.

Unfortunately, work was never far from my thoughts.

We returned to Spike's house following the event and it was clear that I needed a nap. I had outdone myself. The guest room upstairs would be my haven. I hunkered down under the covers listening to the sounds of life, video games, my family, laughter, and love and joy. I was grateful. I was thankful. I was blessed. My family was together and it didn't matter what we did; we could take a nap, read a book, or watch TV, but all we wanted to do was to be in the same house together. We just wanted to know that we had all gotten through the last year and that life would continue.

Monday, December 7, 2009

Someday, I will learn to be careful what I wish for. Life is getting back to normal. *Emails. Phone calls. Standard operating questions.*

I'd been picking up speed.

"Do you have 140 yards of wall covering in stock?"

"Can you please deliver that sample chair on Thursday?"

"What are the power requirements for the special twenty-foot conference table?"

It was like nothing had ever happened. Except that now I had whitish-greyish, curly, short hair—and big scars on my boobs.

On one of these ordinary days, I stopped to grab a cup of coffee with a friend. Seated in the comfy, cozy lounge pieces, we chatted about travel and the bigger world. She was fifteen years my junior and was getting ready to embark on some new and interesting adventures. Her life was just kicking off, she was dreaming of lands far away, and I was intrigued.

"Check out *Idealist.org*," she suggested. "It's pretty awesome. It has volunteer opportunities all over the world in all different capacities."

I scratched IDEALIST into my red leather notebook

"I've also used the *Nomad's Guide to World Travel*. It's this huge reference guide for how to be a smart, economical traveler. It gives pointers on where to go, how to save money, and highlights of areas. I've read it cover to cover."

"Where are you going first?" I asked.

"Not sure. I'm researching and planning and saving. I probably won't go for another year or so, and by that time I'll have an itinerary all hashed out."

Such a thoughtful, organized soul. I was an impulsive, spontaneous, and often ill-prepared traveler. Those planner people were good to have around. I made a mental note about my friend's meticulous nature.

The next morning, while I sat drinking coffee and answering emails, I stared out the window at the snow-covered ground and felt grateful to be out of bed. The coffee tasted superb. The sunlight on my face was heavenly. My cats were snuggled together in my home office. As I tediously opened email after email, I wondered when selling chairs had become the focus of my life again. The daily business calls had piled up and, eventually, I shook my head and asked myself, "How could the person on the other end of the phone be SO NEUROTIC about a desk? A DESK!"

There had to be something more. My fingers typed *Idealist.org* into the search box.

It was a portal into a bigger world. Tabs read: jobs, organizations, and volunteer organizations. That was the one. *Volunteer Organizations.* Click. The new screen was titled *Focus*: children, poverty, agriculture, education, women's business issues, environment, etc. Easy. I clicked on children. The next tab asked me to select a country. The pull-down menu was a mile long. My ignorance screamed at me. I had no idea how to even pronounce some of the names, much less have any idea where they were. I was a geographical dunce.

But the dreaming would have to be put on hold for a bit—someone was screaming in an email about vinyl options for a hospital chair.

Sunday, December 20, 2009

I hung a map of the world where my old cancer calendars had once lived. *Idealist.org* was my new project. Every so often, I daydreamed about other parts of the world, searching different countries on my computer. I printed off home pages of orphanages in Kenya, women's business development opportunities in Rio de Janeiro, and meditation centers in India. The map of the world started to get covered with colorful post-it notes and email addresses and smiley faces.

When the furniture world got claustrophobic, I traveled via computer to an orphanage in Kenya. Images of beautiful children and magnificent landscapes filled my screen. I watched videos of college students in the slums of Nairobi, complete with poverty, desperation, and hopelessness. And then I watched and listened as these same college students took the problem into their own hands and addressed these issues; not by throwing money at the situation, but by changing the paradigm.

These young adults had actually started their own children's home in a rural area of Kenya. Their time was dedicated to improving the well-being of a small number of children in a clean, healthy environment. The message was about quality, not quantity. The goal was to provide exemplary care—the same kind of care we would give our own children. It wasn't just about keeping these children alive. It was about feeding them, housing them, teaching them, and setting them on a path that would then allow them to change their own world. It was idealistic to say the least, and I was hooked.

Chemo had thrown me into early menopause, as I mentioned, which meant that cancer had taken away my ability to create children. However, my maternal instincts were still alive. Although there would be no mini-me, maybe there were other options. As I'd struggled to find meaning in my life, I had started to consider the option that maybe the Big Guy had other plans.

"Get up. Dust yourself off. You've got a second chance. Go do something to help someone else."

It wasn't really a blinking red neon sign screaming at me, but it was close. My internal voice was banging hard on my heart, saying: "Go be with kids. Go try it. Go do it. Just go."

At first, I didn't tell too many people about these ideas or the crazy voices inside my head—for obvious reasons. During an acupuncture session, I was handed a Chinese medicine book about healing breast cancer. Chapter Two was titled: *Change of Lifestyle*. In other words, don't do what you used to. The Chinese believed that there was some negative energy flow from previous lifestyles that instigated growth of cancer. This seemed a little voodoo-ish to me, but my psyche was open to all sorts of input. Even if this wasn't totally the case, I had come to the reality check that cancer may have been my wake-up call. Something was shifting.

I had developed a new sense of connection with the universe and was willing to let it take me where it wanted me to go.

I would not resist. I would not argue. I would listen and be open.

I eventually went to the Hilltop Children's Home website—the one for the children's home in Kenya. I clicked *CONTACT US* and sent an introductory "I'm interested" email. Within hours, I had a response from Jane, the volunteer coordinator.

The conversations had started.

Saturday, December 26, 2009

Although I was physically healthy, Christmas was disturbing this year. My empty house was painfully obvious. There were not a lot of visitors. No kids. No trips to see Santa and the reindeer at the Victorian Stroll. No gingerbread houses or Grinch movies. No stringing popcorn. Nope. My Christmas had become a pre-strung, three-piece, snap-together plastic tree and two red felt stockings in the shapes of cat paws.

A sadness existed deep in my soul and wouldn't go away, just like the fear that my cancer would come back. Coming to terms with reality was pushing me out of my comfort zone. Random TV shows, books, and websites had me bouncing around the world, though. I could go to Ecuador to visit an alternative cancer doctor. The children's home in Kenya spoke to my maternal instincts. An ashram in India shouted *PEACE* at me. I felt like I needed to do something different, to shatter my view of normal.

I was on a collision course with my own destiny.

Monday, March 1, 2010

Life had returned to furniture. And a few trips to the plastic surgeon to have my expanders expanded and create fake boobs in my chest, of course. I sold chairs, conference tables, and fabric day after day. I negotiated with myself and my dreams and acceptance.

The standard three-month follow-up happened two weeks ago. It was a battery of tests which consisted of a liver X-ray and some other innocuous scans and bloodwork. Waiting for results was like sitting on a pin cushion and trying to act like it didn't hurt.

Is it gone? Do I have cancer still/again? Please don't make me go through this again. I hope I did everything right. I hope I don't have cancer. I hope I don't have cancer. I hope I don't have cancer.

These are the obsessive, compulsive, non-stop thoughts that go through a survivor's brain during testing time. Yet, "normal" life continues.

By Friday of that week, the nurse and I had traded off turns at playing phone tag three times. It was important that I talked to her before she left for the day. A weekend without answers was going to throw me into a crazy, bed-ridden, insane forty-eight hours. I was being proactive—if not obsessive and aggressive.

Fuck it. Self-care comes in all forms.

"Bethany, it's Donna. Please call me when you can."

By five-thirty at night, I sat stone-cold on the kitchen floor staring at the phone, waiting for it to ring. Waiting. Waiting. Waiting. At six o'clock, the bouncy ring tone jolted me and I banged at the *Answer* button when I saw the hospital's caller ID.

"Hello?"

"Hey, Bethany. It's Donna."

"Hey, Donna. Tell me everything is fine," I declared. I had no interest in being pleasant. I was too nervous, too anxious.

"Well, the bloodwork looks good, but there is something suspicious on your liver. We see a spot."

To my own surprise, I didn't faint, pass out, or stop breathing.

Suspicious. Stupid fucking word.

Shit. Shit. Shit.

I had to listen.

"It's probably nothing, but we need to do more tests."

I had nothing to say. Donna told me about where and when my next set of tests would take place.

"Okay. Thanks," I muttered, and then I hung up the phone.

I immediately rolled into the fetal position and talked to the Big Guy.

"Thy will be done," I repeated over and over again, wrapping my arms around my knees as I lay on the white and green linoleum tile. "Thy will be done. Thy will be done."

The following week, I returned to the hospital for more tests. Day after day, I was poked and prodded.

Results came back and the spot on my liver ended up being nothing. "A false positive" was what they call it.

However, my pancreas was enlarged.

My pancreas? WTF?

I moved into researcher mode. I did a quick web search about pancreatic cancer. Not good. Pancreatic cancer wasn't one of the better cancers to have. Things weren't looking

good, so I stayed home. I didn't talk to people. I *avoided*…
everything. I didn't answer my phone. I didn't go to work.
I sat and watched TV, waiting for results in the ugly green
velour recliner with my cats sitting on my lap.

Marie showed up at my house. I let her in. She
understood. She refused to let me isolate myself in my
fear and anxiety, though. She coaxed me out of the house.
We drove for hours, went to the movies, took a pottery
class, and ate lots of good food and tons of ice cream. The
hours passed and we laughed and joked and cried and
talked about God. Nothing was resolved, but I hadn't been
catatonic in a corner for days. This was why I loved this
woman.

Saturday, March 6, 2010

After another week of panic-ridden existence mixed with various upholstery fabrics and wood finishes, Nurse Donna called.

"All clean," she declared. "You are fine. Everything is good."

I said… "Thanks."

That's it? It was over?

It wasn't over. It was never going to be over. It was always going to be there. The false positive results had catapulted me into a world beyond my typical imagination. For three weeks, I had questioned my life. I had questioned my death. I'd pondered my legacy, and now I found profound gratitude and an unexplainable fearlessness.

Through this time, my thought process had always returned to the same question. "What do I want my life to look like? What am I supposed to be doing?"

And then it came to me. In a nice, serene, soft way, I was reminded of what I already knew. I wanted peace and serenity. I wanted to feel complete. I wanted to know that I had lived my life with a purpose. I wanted to know that I had done something meaningful. My motherless-ness left a hole inside me…. No legacy. No next generation. No mini-me to play dress-up with or bring to school or hug and kiss and read stories to at night.

Nope. That wasn't my story.

But I was being given a second chance… a do-over.

I clicked away at the keyboard. I visited the website again. Hilltop Children's Home. The children's home in

Naivasha, Kenya. Julianne had sent me basic information about how the program worked: how many children lived at the house and what volunteers did. Pictures on the website showed clean, smiling children holding hands and running through fields. Tears came unexpectedly and a wave of contentment came over my body. I knew in my gut that this was exactly the right thing to do.

The wall that used to have calendars full of doctor appointments and phone numbers had been transformed into a "Get to Kenya" wall. The map of the world was covered with lists of what to pack, shots needed, and the names of the kids in Kenya.

My furniture job was going to take a back seat. Large sales were getting kicked to the curb. Money was not driving the bus anymore. I did not have cancer—my tests were clear, and I was opting out of materialism. A sense of faith and security filled my being. Peace and serenity were settling in. I was making a conscious decision on how to live my life. I needed to get outside myself and help others.

Wednesday, March 17, 2010

Decision made! I was going to Kenya to live with thirteen children.

As I enthusiastically told my parents about the plans for my upcoming adventure, my dad grumped, "You won't be there long enough to make a difference. Only long enough to get in trouble."

I ignored his comment.

The next day, I called Spike to vent. He was the only person I knew who had been to a developing country and might understand.

"Daddy thinks I'm crazy. He doesn't think ten weeks will make a difference." I wanted my father to be proud of me.

"You *will* make a difference," Spike said firmly. "Any amount of time you spend there will matter. Even if it was just a week. It's good for you. Just go."

I love my brother.

Thursday, March 18, 2010

The volunteer packet was complete with all the significant information needed to assist people with their transition into Kenya. There was a packing list as well as basic background data for travelers: required shots, currency exchanges, and suggested donations for the children.

The Hilltop Children's Home was located in Naivasha, a small village at the foothills of the Aberdare Mountains in central Kenya. The home was powered by a kerosene generator in the evenings so that the children could study. Drinking water needed to be boiled or purchased as bottled water. The children in the home ranged from four to fifteen years old, and the organization's goal was to provide a family lifestyle as best it possibly could.

My father's cynicism would infiltrate my optimistic and excited thought process in the weeks leading up to the trip. *What if I get to Nairobi and there's no one at the airport to pick me up? What if this is just a scam and they just want my money? What if I get stranded in the middle of East Africa by myself?*

Could I be that naïve? Yep, I'm pretty sure I could be.

I'd had a few conversations with Jane, the volunteer coordinator for Hilltop Children's Home. She seemed pleasant enough, but if this was a scam, then she could just be a plant, too. It could all just be one big conspiracy. I sent more emails. I asked more questions. I asked for references. I was not a world traveler at all, and yet I was committed to going to Kenya.

I probably should have been committed to a mental health unit at the local hospital.

Nevertheless, I was full of neurotic questions and uncertainties. Eventually, Jane had Charlie, one of the founders of the organization, call me. His strong British accent caught me off-guard when I answered the phone.

"Hi. This is Charlie Wilson of Hilltop Children's Home."

What did he say? He was speaking English, wasn't he?

"Charlie. From Hilltop Children's Home."

I had to pay close attention to his words.

"Jane said you might have some questions."

I stuttered a bit, trying to collect my thoughts. "Yeah, well, I just want to make sure someone will pick me up at the airport, and that it's safe where the house is. And that the money will get used for the kids."

He answered my questions quickly in that foreign English language, and somehow, by the time I got off the phone, I realized I was about to enter another world—a world where everything was different and people were diverse. I was going to get to meet new people and get a fresh perspective on life. I was going to live with a bunch of kids and maybe tutor them and help them and bring them some clothes and socks and shoes.

Cancer wasn't on my radar anymore.

Wednesday, April 14, 2010

This morning, I snuggled in bed with my cats. I'll be leaving them again soon. Punky sprawled across my chest, licking my face. Mazey cuddled alongside me and purred. They're getting shipped to my parents' house again. Their grandparents.

I knew I wasn't right in the head. It wasn't like I was leaving a husband or a boyfriend or actual children. They were my cats. Cats! I sighed. And yet there was something so wonderful about these furry black and white lovebugs. I always knew where they were. I always knew that they loved me. They were unconditional creatures that kept me semi-sane, and I would miss them. I knew my niece Cheyenne would love them and cuddle with them while I was gone.

And I knew I would be homesick, but I had to do this. I had to go.

Sunday, April 18, 2010

Last night, I made the trip into New York City for a Hilltop Children's Home fundraiser. I met Charlie, the guy with the British accent—who, by the look of his youthful face, is probably only thirty years old. I met Jane, the volunteer coordinator I've spoken with numerous times. She has long, red curly hair and appears to be maybe twenty-five years old. I was also introduced to Susan Milford, the Country Director who would be living at the house in Kenya while I was there.

Susan was a Georgetown Law School student. Following graduation, she had practiced in Manhattan for a year. It wasn't as fulfilling as she expected. She also had looked for something more meaningful, so she quit and agreed to donate a year of her time to Hilltop Children's Home. Susan would be meeting me at the airport when I arrive in Nairobi. We chatted about what to expect and about the growth potential at Hilltop Children's Home. We talked about the kids and the food and about potential fundraising. I was pleasantly surprised to learn there was a bathroom at the house.

It was a far cry from talking about tables and chairs.

Monday, April 26, 2010

The generosity of others continues to amaze me.

On Saturday, a group of furniture friends gathered at my home. Each of them came with bags and boxes of donations for the children in Naivasha. They were equipped with packing supplies and duct tape and hand-written love letters from their own children. They had shopped for pants and sweaters and blouses and dresses and school supplies and shoes. Underwear and books and toys and glow sticks filled the boxes. It was a machine! The group of givers packaged, weighed, and labeled ten boxes with HILLTOP CHILDREN'S HOME, NAIVASHA, KENYA. Big yellow smiley faces were plastered on the sides and the boxes were stacked in my van. Six hundred pounds of stuff would travel with me to Nairobi.

Monday, May 3, 2010

Crossing the Atlantic Ocean was uneventful, but torturously long. Seven hours, to be exact. Economy seat. Middle section. Middle row. Cramped legs. Head-nods. Slight drooling episodes.

Long distance travel wasn't quite as exciting and glamorous as I had envisioned.

London. Heathrow Airport. Terminal three. An airport version of Rodeo Drive mixed with world travelers shopping at Versace, Burberry, Armani, and Cartier. People were meticulously coiffed with perfect makeup, flawless skin, and an obviously high-end attitude. Shiny shop walls sparkled like diamonds. The British accents stunned my ears as I made my way through hallways of opulence, giving my legs some much needed movement. A Starbucks soy vanilla latte helped jolt me back into the land of the living. Rows of contemporary high-back, black leather seats invited me to pull out my book and settle in for the show. I scanned the chairs, the stores, the people, the carpet, and the lighting fixtures, and sipped away at my latte, relishing the fact that I was actually in London. *Fancy.*

An unattended brown knapsack sitting near a phonebooth caught my attention. Airport security warnings rang through my brain. *"Do not leave your bags unattended."* Booming alarms inside me made the hair on my arms stand at full attention. Hundreds of other travelers passed by with zero interest. Those announcements about notifying security of suspicious activity banged away at my peace of mind. For an hour, my eyes darted between the bag, the phonebooth, the tourists, and my book. Surely, someone else would do something.

Eventually, the phone at the phonebooth started to ring and a middle-aged man who looked to be from the Middle East showed up from out of nowhere, picked up the handset, and carried on a short conversation.

Oh shit. This was like a movie. Maybe I had watched too much *Law and Order* and *NCIS*. My brain screamed "Tell someone!" I considered emailing my brother. I could let him know what was going on.... Just in case the airport blew up while I was in it. I took a few deep breaths, and watched the man replace the handset and walk away. The bag was left on the floor. It was still there at the end of my twelve-hour layover. There were no SWAT teams, no exploding terminals... just my vivid imagination getting carried away. I would eventually come to learn how much the America media had created my thought processes and therefore my prejudices. This was just the beginning.

Hours later, I boarded Virgin Atlantic Flight 671 and settled in for the next nine hours, hoping that I wouldn't drool on the old lady in the seat next to me.

As we got closer to Nairobi, I made my way to the bathroom and removed cash from the tan elastic safety pouch that was strapped around my belly. All the travel books talked about that. *Keep money close to your person. Don't flash bills around.* I was being vigilant for once and doing what the book said. I shoved $200 in my front pocket, made my way back to my seat, and took a deep breath. I was almost in Africa. Kenya, to be exact. It was a long way from home, but I wasn't that scared. My heart of hearts told me I was doing the right thing. I just knew it.

The first order of business when arriving in Nairobi was to figure out the money situation. Small currency exchange kiosks were located along the wall in the baggage claim area. People yelled at me from behind the windows with bars.

"Mama! Mama! Get your money here!"

I tentatively approached one of the windows and handed a man $200 in exchange for shillings. He returned to me a stack of yellow, red, and green bills. 16,750 Kenyan shillings. I probably should have figured out the exchange rate in advance, but even if I'd known what the rate was, I would have had no idea what it meant. I was a naive traveler. My blonde hair and whiter-than-pale skin practically screamed "ignorant tourist." They had to know.

Around the corner, coming down the cargo shoot, were my twelve cardboard boxes with big yellow smiley faces on them. Yesterday, these smiley faces had seemed so cute when we'd been loading the plane at JFK. Here, they seemed rather obnoxious and out of place.

Three young men standing around the baggage area saddled up next to me. They began speaking to me, but not in English.

Shit, I thought, *what the hell have I gotten into? I thought people spoke English here.*

Cargo carts were corralled in the corner. I pulled one out and wheeled it to the conveyor. The men nodded as I pointed out yellow smiley face after yellow smile face. One after another, the boxes were stacked on the metal carts. Three men, three carts, and 600 pounds of stuff made its way to the exit lane.

The customs lady was about six feet tall, with broad shoulders and a heavy, furrowed brow. Her stark, navy blue suit and intimidating demeanor made me feel uncertain.

"What is in these boxes?" she asked sternly with a bold British accent.

"Gifts for children at an orphanage." I smiled back at her, hoping my bubbly personality would win her over.

"What kind of gifts?" she replied, scrutinizing me.

"Clothes. Books. Toys."

"New or used?"

"Used," I lied.

Something about this woman made me want to crawl into a hole. Something made me believe that it would be better if they were used. I don't have a very good poker face, though, and she knew it was a fib from the second I opened my mouth.

"Open the boxes," she ordered her assistant.

The cardboard boxes were filled with shoes, shirts, stuffed animals, books, and underwear, all nicely packed and newly purchased, with their tags visibly hanging off.

What happens now? Are they going to send me home? Why did I lie? What is going on?

"Did you register all this with the government?" She looked down her nose at me.

"No. These are donations for the children here. I'm here to help. I don't know anything about registering with the government."

"You do realize that by bringing these goods into the country, there are many shop owners who will not make a profit. You are circumventing potential business in our country. You need to pay taxes."

This aspect had never occurred to me. Circumventing their economy by bringing donations? I'd thought I was doing something good. Our conversation was causing some commotion—or maybe it was the excess amount of baggage or the yellow smiley faces.

Her manager arrived at what was starting to feel like a check-out line at the grocery store.

"How much? How much would the taxes be?" I asked in my usual loud voice.

Everyone started to stammer and look back and forth at each other. I didn't understand.

"This time, we will let you through," the manager said politely. "Next time, however, you need to talk to the Department of Children Affairs and fill out the necessary paperwork."

"Okay. Okay. Sorry about that. I didn't know the protocol. I'll pay attention next time."

Drivers lined the exit, holding placards with names on them. Big men who looked angry. They were staring at me, or at least that's what my ego-centric, self-absorbed version of events thought. A blonde, white woman with yellow smiley-face boxes who had no clue what she was doing. I probably smelled of fear. I walked up and down the sidewalk, my anxiety rising. No one had my name. I didn't know how to use my phone. I didn't know about country codes or how to call the USA or this country's version of 911 in case of emergency. *It was probably in that volunteer handbook. Maybe I should have paid more attention to it.*

The porters looked at me with confusion on their faces. I shrugged at them as we wheeled the luggage outside and found a spot along the wall to sit and wait. Billboards of safari outfits with pictures of lions, zebras, and giraffes dotted the corridor. Vending machines offered bottled water and Coca Cola. Kiosks touted cold ice cream and sweets. Businessmen moved briskly through the area. Cars were coming and going. Police officers directed the traffic. I waited and watched. I looked at the guys standing next to me and smiled. Or, at least, I tried to smile.

"Bethany!" From across the parking lot, two men yelled my name as they approached our group and handed me a cell phone.

"Hello?" I answered as I looked at the newest strangers standing in front of me.

"Hey," said Susan, the woman I had met in New York. "We're running late, but the driver will take care of you. His name is Anthony. I'm going to drop off Heather, another volunteer, in two minutes. So sorry. We were stuck in traffic. We're on our way."

Anthony took the phone and shook my hand. His smile was warm and friendly.

"Jambo. Welcome to Kenya. So sorry we are late."

"Thank you so much for meeting me. I'm Bethany."

My anxiety level took a nose dive. Anthony started an animated conversation in Swahili with the porters as we made our way to the parking lot. Boxes were quickly shoved into a green Land Rover and the dialogue between the men seemed to escalate. It was the tone…. Something was happening.

Back and forth. One of the porters. The driver. Another porter. Hands flailing. Pointing from the terminal to the truck and back again.

After a few minutes, Anthony turned to me and said, "You need to tip them each one hundred and fifty shillings."

I nodded and dug out the wad of what seemed like Monopoly money, and then I flipped through looking for the correct denominations. Bills were dispersed as the porters grumbled and muttered and shoved the money in their pockets and walked away. One hundred and fifty shillings. Translation? $1.75 U.S. dollars. I had heard about negotiating for everything, but hadn't realized that it happened with every transaction. Lesson number one? Never pay full price. Lesson number two? Don't show wads of cash in public. Duh. I was so ignorant and out of my element.

Within minutes, another vehicle pulled up to our side. Susan's familiar face was a welcome relief. She greeted me with a big hug and introduced me to blonde-haired, blue-eyed Heather, another volunteer.

"Sorry we're late, but there's lots going on," Susan said breathlessly. She proceeded to explain that Heather would be traveling with me to Naivasha because she had meetings to attend. Meetings? They had meetings in Kenya? I was so ignorant.

Heather was about 5'4" and appeared to be about twenty years old. She had lived at Hilltop Children's Home for a few months and was very familiar with the town and the drivers, spurting out cultural information as we made our way onto the highway. My lack of sleep was catching up to me and a headache was starting to develop between my eyeballs. A distinct and unfamiliar smell infiltrated my nostrils.

Heather eagerly pointed out Kibera on our left. "It's the largest slum in Africa. It's about the size of Central Park in New York. They say a million people live there."

For miles, we passed homes crafted of timber and scrap metal walls. Corrugated metal sheets completed the structures, acting as roofs. There were no windows—just timber doors left open for light. House after house after house. The most prevalent color was brown, the same color as the dirt on the ground, but shops were painted in bright blues and greens and yellows. Billboards advertised Nivea and Coca Cola and Safaricom.

The roads in the city had been paved, but the driver consistently switched lanes back and forth to avoid potholes the size of small craters that would undoubtedly have done damage to his vehicle. There were no yellow or white lines painted on the roads and traffic was chaotic. Piles of garbage smoldered on the sides of the streets. Donkeys and cows pulled carts. Waste mixed with water flowed in the ditches. Young girls carried babies in colorful pouches on their backs. Older women had baskets on their heads. Men in dark suits were walking home from work. It smelled of dirt and diesel and waste. The dust stuck to my face. I squeezed my eyes to stop the burning tears. *Overload.* This was definitely overload.

As we made our way out of the city and towards the rural village of Naivasha, the houses became more sporadic. The population started to dwindle, and the air smelled less like diesel. Pom-pom type trees dotted the landscape and green rolling hills led us through the countryside.

Heather talked about Bruce, another volunteer who had been at the house for three weeks, and about the Magnet Effect, the Oasis program, and about all the meetings she had to attend. I tried to keep up with everything she was saying, but most of it went in one ear and out the other.

We dodged random cows and donkeys on the road. People carried firewood on their backs and children didn't have shoes, but the atmosphere seemed calmer, more simplistic, the further we went.

Mile after mile, I watched the scenery pass. I was actually in Kenya. In Africa. Squished in a Land Rover full of boxes of donations headed to an orphanage in a town that I had never heard of three months before. Buses and motorbikes whizzed by.

Forty-five minutes outside of Nairobi, Anthony pointed to the left and said, "The Great Rift Valley."

"What's that? How did that happen?" I asked as I looked at what appeared to be a lowland.

Anthony was obviously very proud of this geological site.

"Plate tectonics. Twenty million years ago, the plates pulled apart and the ground dropped. The valley runs the length of most of East Africa."

Wow. My education with plate tectonics had always been about the formation of mountains, or at least that's what I remembered. I had never given thought to what happened on the other side of the plates. Of course, a valley would be created. Just another perspective. We stopped and took photos, but they would never do the amazing scene justice.

A hour and a half after leaving Nairobi, we arrived at the junction in Naivasha. There was a gas station on one corner, a strip mall on the other, and a bus stop strategically placed at the intersection. It was a busy town with lots of activity in every direction. Logos for Safaricom, Yu, and Zain were plastered on the brightly colored shops. We passed timber-constructed kiosks full of white plastic buckets neatly stacked full of potatoes. Dresses and blouses hung from the open timbers, swaying in the wind. Butchery windows had sides of beef hanging for all to see. Hand-made signs for internet cafés, salons, and schools were passed by. *Where am I?* I wondered. We veered to the right, down a hill, over a bridge, and back up the other side. People were walking everywhere, up and down hills, taking shortcuts through riverbanks and in and out of alleyways. Donkeys pulled carts full of cabbage. Men walked around carrying machetes. *I need to breathe.* Children in matching school uniforms and tattered shoes, carrying bags full of books, made their way along the roads. Anthony made a left onto a dirt road at the green and white sign labeled *KCB Bank.*

Heather seemed unphased by the rough ride up the treacherous, muddy riverbed of a road. I swallowed hard to keep my stomach in place. *Don't get sick. Don't do it.*

As we crested the top of the hill, a wooden gate was opened by a stocky, smiling man with a knife strapped to his hip. An assembly of thirteen children, two older women, and a young white man were neatly arranged as the greeting committee out front. I gently removed myself from the vehicle and stood in awe at the cohesive group.

"Hi, Bethany. I'm Bruce. We're so glad you're here." The fair-skinned, blonde-haired young man shook my hand and gently put his arm around my shoulder. Bruce's six-foot frame and smiling blue eyes offered me a sense of strength and comfort. He stood next to me as the children began singing "The Welcome Song."

The kids ranged widely in height and age, and as I looked into each of their faces, I was overcome with a new reality. These were just normal kids meeting another grown-up. They formed a line, and each child shook my hand and introduced him or herself to me. They were polite, clean, and made eye contact, and, to my surprise, most of their English was very good. They called me Auntie Bethany.

One by one, I began to put faces to the names. Josh, Matthew, Margaret, Lynn, Helen, Jim, Jamie, Ava, Billy, Leonard, Adam, David, Charlotte. *Thirteen kids. That's a lot of kids to live in one house,* I thought as I was swept up in the moment.

When the formalities were complete, Bruce spoke to two of the older girls. "Why don't you give Auntie Bethany a tour of the house?"

Ava and Charlotte smiled brightly and grabbed my hands. They laced their fingers with mine and walked me in the direction of the sprawling stone house.

Thirteen-year-old Charlotte had a natural beauty that radiated from the inside out. Her slender frame, high cheekbones, and shaved head should have been on the cover of a magazine someplace. Her almond-shaped eyes smiled and danced.

"We are so glad you are here, Auntie. Where are you from?"

"New York," I replied.

"Oh. America. It's so far."

I nodded my head in agreement.

Ava was a smaller version of Charlotte, also thin and with a bald head. Her tiny features reminded me of a Kewpie doll. If I hadn't known better, I would have thought they were biological sisters.

The girls led me towards the green door of the sprawling stone home. It resembled an old English cottage with red roof tiles and eight pane windows strategically placed to allow maximum light into the dwelling. As we made our way into the house, our first stop was the volunteer area—a room similar to a college lounge that came complete with two loveseats and two big, cushy chairs. A four-burner stove was attached to an orange propane tank and the sink was nicely placed in front of a bay of windows overlooking the entrance to the compound. There were shelves for food, and a table stacked with fresh fruit and eggs in a wire basket shaped like a chicken. The girls showed me the bathroom, which was actually two rooms; one was just a toilet room, and the other had the tub (with no showerhead) and a sink. I was relieved to discover there was running water. We made our way down the hallway, each girl telling me about their day at school, who their teacher was, and what their favorite subject was.

"This is your room," Charlotte said as she showed me a bedroom with two separate bunkbeds compactly placed inside.

There was a five-drawer dresser, a bookcase acting as shelves for clothes, and bright red plaid curtains lining the windows. It looked like people were actually living out of the suitcases strewn about the floor, and the long table was cluttered with a power strip, laptops, chargers, and cameras.

Nivea skin cream, sunscreen, and crayon-colored pictures filled the rest of the table.

"Isn't it wonderful?" Charlotte asked.

"I love it," I replied, not knowing proper etiquette for the situation.

Ava tugged at my hand. "Come see our room!" she squealed.

I was pulled into a vast room with five metal bunkbeds placed around the walls. The beds were neatly made with pink sheets tucked in at the corners, each one complete with a pink pillow and a stuffed animal propped up against it. It was a happy room full of windows and light, and hand-drawn pictures were taped to the white-painted walls.

"This is my bed!" Ava declared enthusiastically as she climbed to the top of one of the bunks and grabbed hold of a brown bear. "Auntie Mombi gave me this teddy."

She then scurried off the bed and pulled at my hand. "Look here. This is my box."

A stack of blue metal boxes was located next to the closet. Each box had a girl's name written on it with colorful stickers and drawings on the front. She lifted the lid of her box and pulled out a hand-written letter on a piece of blue paper.

"My sponsor wrote me a letter. See? And she sent me some nail polish, too."

I quickly realized that this three-foot by two-foot blue metal box held all the important items in Ava's life. Everything in one box.

The boys' room was identical to the girls' room in every way except the colors. Instead of pink sheets and pillows, theirs were blue. In place of flower drawings and girly stickers, they had hand-drawn pictures of trucks and airplanes. As I peeked in, Charlotte introduced me to Billy and Adam, who were sitting on the wood floor racing their matchbox cars back and forth. They both acknowledged my existence, smiled politely, and went back to their green and yellow sports cars.

Ava positioned herself beside me and tugged at my hand. She led me to the darkly paneled sitting room. The fireplace was opposite the wall of windows and the smell of last night's blaze hung in the air. A sofa, loveseat, and lounge chair were all upholstered in a blue speckled material with an accent strip of rust fabric wrapped around the wooden arms. I resisted the sudden reflex to flip the chairs and walked further into the room with Ava.

A forty-two-inch flat-screen TV was the focal point of the room, nicely displayed on a long storage cabinet. A flat-screen TV? Now that was a big surprise.

"This is where we come after dinner each night," said Ava. "We all sit around and talk about our day and about school and watch a movie."

Next, Ava showed me the dining room, which was complete with a seemingly never-ending wooden table and benches on either side. Two women appeared from yet another hallway and introduced themselves.

"Good day, I'm Phoebe," said the older of the two as her strong hands enclosed mine.

"And I'm Joyce," the younger lady said with an outstretched hand and a dazzling smile.

Both women were wearing long skirts, blouses, and black dress shoes. *Why are they so dressed up?* I wondered.

"Ava," said Phoebe. "It's time to wash your socks and shoes. Go with the others."

Ava hopped off down the hallway.

"Come," Phoebe said to me.

I followed her down a narrow hallway with rickety floorboards and stone walls.

"Let's have tea. You must be tired."

The kitchen was equipped with three gas burners, wooden shelves stacked with metal bowls, and blue and red plastic mugs imprinted with the letters OK on them. A leopard-print upholstered bench was neatly situated under the window that faced the yard full of children and a packed clothesline.

"Uncle Peter just bought us this bench," Joyce said with a smile, nodding to it. "They carried it up the hill from town this morning. It's so smart, don't you think? Sit down. Sit."

I sat and watched as Joyce and Phoebe went about preparing tea. Children were running past the window and the sounds of laughter filled the room. A tiny boy with big eyes and a dripping nose entered the kitchen.

"Billy, go fetch us some milk from the down kitchen," said Phoebe.

"Yes, Mom," he replied, and off he went.

Mom?

When Billy returned with a bucket of steaming milk, Joyce deftly added scoops of tealeaves and sugar, stirred the concoction, and finally poured it through a strainer into a blue plastic mug. I raised it to my lips and was delighted with a taste that was nothing short of decadent. *Bingo. If nothing else, I can drink this for ten weeks.*

Both women pulled up chairs beside me and started chatting with me like we were all old friends.

I learned that Phoebe was the eldest of the matrons and had been with Hilltop Children's Home since its inception. She was married with eight children of her own. She lived on the "other side" of town, the side past the river.

Joyce was in her mid-thirties, a single mom whose only son Sylvester was a day scholar at the Hilltop Children's Home school. I was surprised to learn these women had their own families, and yet their full-time job was taking care of other people's children. The dynamics had never crossed my mind, but that may have been because I'd never been a mother.

As I sat in the small room sipping chai, the exhaustion started to sink in.

"Where is my room again?" I asked. "What time is it? What am I supposed to be doing?"

Before either Joyce or Phoebe could reply, Bruce magically appeared to escort me back to the room that would become my home for the next ten weeks.

"Just rest." His kind voice calmed me. "Take all the time you need. Sleep in tomorrow. We'll all be here when you wake up."

I didn't argue. Happily, I climbed into a bottom bunk and rested my head on the lumpy pillow. As usual, I hadn't put two and two together when doing my minimal preparation. Being at an altitude of 8,000 feet means it's usually cooler than in areas down the mountain. I was grateful for the red and blue and green plaid blankets that covered the beds. At least I would be warm. I pulled the wool blankets over my head and listened to kids talking in a strange language outside the window. As I closed my eyes, my mind was bombarded with troubling thoughts:

There is no way I am going to be able to do this. No way. It's too different. I'm too different. They don't like me. I'm too old. It's too scary. Ten weeks? WHAT was I thinking?

I crafted a quick email to friends and family on my Blackberry, letting them know I had arrived safely, popped an Ambien, and slowly faded away.

Tuesday, May 4, 2010

Surprisingly, the bunkbed was fairly comfortable, or maybe it was the two days of travel, the seven-hour time difference, and the Ambien that helped. I probably could have slept on a cement floor and thought that was comfy, too.

A strong male voice speaking what I hoped was Swahili jolted me from my sleep. *What time is it? Is it morning? Why is there a man here? What was he saying?* He'd sounded angry.

Two small, lively voices responded to the deep, dark tone, and then they were all gone. My fears subsided.

As I opened my eyes, I scanned the surroundings. Long strips of wood were directly located above my head, holding the above mattress in place. It had been a long time since I had slept in a bunkbed, probably back when I was in college—like all the other volunteers here, I imagined. The room was dark, and I rolled over in bed trying to escape my troubling thoughts.

This is insane. You have completely lost your mind. Dad was right. You can't make a difference here. The problems are just too big. Just stay in bed. Don't leave this compound—ever. All those people in town will not like you. They will be mad that you are white. They will beg for money and chase you screaming down the street. Stay here at Hilltop Children's Home for ten weeks. Stay behind the gates. Just play with the kids. That's what you came here for anyway.

I sulked and cried and wondered when the next flight to New York left.

Hours later, I pulled myself out of bed and stood in the bedroom, prodding myself to actually walk out into the next room. I cracked open the door and the sunlight made me squint. At my feet was a folded piece of white paper with a hand-drawn calla lily etched on the front. Written inside was a letter from Bruce.

"Good Morning, Bethany! You made it through day one and today is shaping up to be a beautiful day two. We are so happy you are here and are all at your beck-and-call to answer questions and make you feel at home in this rewarding place. Enjoy the day! We'll see you tonight. Always—Bruce, Heather, and Susan."

I hugged the piece of paper close to my chest and walked towards the volunteer room. Through the hallway windows, a huge mountain filled the blue morning sky. Small stone buildings dotted the green grass yard. Children were scattered about chasing soccer balls, playing jumprope, and reading books. It looked like there were a hundred of them, all dressed in grey sweaters and dark shorts. There was laughter and joy filling the air.

It was a normal school day.

I would later learn that kids from the "other side" of town were transported to our complex for school, grades one through four. Hilltop Children's Home was a community resource, educating more than just its own population of children.

As I took a deep breath and entered the volunteer room, I found that Bruce and Heather were sipping tea and chatting about what kids needed to be tutored that day, what the tasks were, and who was going where in the afternoon.

"Good morning," came a chipper greeting from Bruce.

Everyone turned to look at me standing awkwardly in the doorway.

"I hope you had a good night's sleep." He grinned.

I grunted some type of reply, totally unsure how to answer and feeling very old and very out of place. I sat down next to Bruce just as Joyce entered the room to place a metal tub on the table.

"Jambo!" She smiled at me.

I nodded back at her with a grin, assuming whatever she'd said meant *hello*. Heather lifted the lid on the tub and stared inside.

"Lentils and rice for lunch. *Asante Sana.*"

A tall, sturdy man entered the room to talk to Bruce.

"Auntie, this is Wombogo. Wombogo, this is Bethany," Bruce said. I stood up and shook the hand of this smiling man, assuming he was who I'd heard outside my room earlier.

"Jambo. We are glad you are here." Wombogo's eyes danced.

"Me, too," I lied as the two men left the room to discuss vehicle repairs.

Across from me, Heather and Susan had shifted their discussion from daily activities to the topic of an upcoming event. The Day of the African Child. I listened intently, trying to keep up with what they were saying and quickly coming to the conclusion that there was a celebration being planned. I scooped a ladle full of rice and lentils into a bowl and parked myself on the loveseat again, staring blankly into space and realizing I had never eaten lentils before. I ate them anyway, tasting nothing.

I'm too old, too uptight, and too scared for this. I don't know anything about being a mother. I probably wasn't even completely sane when I decided to come here. I'm in Africa. IN AFRICA.... I shook my head and wondered how I had actually made it this far in life.

After inhaling the bland food, I stood in front of the sink that was full of dirty dishes. *Maybe I can just wash the dishes until I get my sea legs under me. Yes, that would be helpful.* I rolled up my sleeves and started to dig in.

It didn't take me long to realize that there was a reason the sink was full. Doing the dishes was a feat unto itself. The water needed to be boiled, which meant the stove needed to be turned on, which meant the gas tank needed to be turned on. The knobs didn't work, so a set of pliers was used to turn the switch. *Shit.* I'd just wanted to wash a couple of plates and cups. I'd just wanted to be useful. Instead, I had to ask for help every step of the way. I didn't know how to function in this world. Elbows deep in soapsuds, I gazed out the window in front of the sink into the yard, watching as the children played.

"Auntie, Auntie. Look at me!" Billy had bounced in front of the window. He hoisted himself onto the short stone wall that housed a flowerbed and pretended it was a balance beam.

"See, Auntie? See?" He beamed proudly.

"You are so talented!" I cheered through the window. "Very good."

He made his way slowly along the eight-foot span of the wall, dismounted with a big smile, and ran away. My heart hurt. Like all the kids here, this wide-eyed boy, full of energy and life, had no parents, no family. Nothing. And this beautiful, bouncing barrel of energy was HIV positive. He had been found as an infant abandoned in the forest, next to his toddler brother who had passed away from neglect. How could this be?

During my initial introduction to the organization there had been discussion about some of the existing conditions of the children. Learning about their stories and about their health issues were all taken in stride in this environment. Everyone came to the house with their own version of suffering and the family unit worked to support each child in the best possible way. There were connections to doctors in Nairobi which dispensed ARV drugs for the HIV kids free of charge as long as they could be transported to the clinic. Often times, the cost of the bus ride into town was prohibitive to families.

A soft hand touched my shoulder as I stared out the window, my hands mindlessly moving the sponge over a plastic plate. Bruce's face was cheerful and relaxed.

"How are you?" he asked.

Unable to control myself, tears welled up in my eyes and I said, "I don't think I can do this. It's too much. I don't belong here. I don't fit in."

"There's a steep learning curve. But it's quick. Give it a week. Don't worry. You don't have to do this alone."

Who was this young man and how did he know exactly what I'd needed to hear?

I nodded my head in agreement, choked back my emotions, and finished the dishes.

There was always a lot to do in order to run a house with thirteen kids. Susan was busy keeping up with the pace, and she asked if I would help organize the donations. Oh yeah. I had forgotten about all those smiley-face boxes. They'd been whisked away and put into storage during my arrival.

"We didn't want the kids to see all the boxes. They will get what they need when they need it. We don't want to spoil them," she said, grinning. "Joyce will help you. Maybe we give each child one new outfit for now. Is that alright with you?"

I was happy to have something to do. "Sure," I said with a nod.

That afternoon, while all the kids were in school, I found Joyce and Phoebe sitting in the kitchen picking away at a tray full of small brown beans with the radio playing in the background.

Joyce was a beautiful woman with flawless skin and meticulously braided hair. Her cheery accent and warm smile comforted me. The floor-length black skirt and baby blue button-up blouse were form-fitting, and she looked every bit the vision of a teacher from my younger days.

"Hello, Auntie Bethany. How do you feel today?" Both Joyce and Phoebe—or "Mom" as the kids lovingly addressed her—smiled at me as I entered the room.

"Better. I needed the rest."

They nodded and picked at the beans. "We are so happy you are here. God sent you. We just know it." Mom's smiling eyes met mine.

Uh Oh. My soft, secret heart was immediately exposed. I was caught off-guard and chose to ignore the statement.

"Susan suggested that we sort out the boxes this afternoon. Can you help me?"

"Yes. Yes. I'd be happy to help."

Joyce jumped up, passed the rattan tray full of beans to Mom, and straightened her skirt. "The boxes are in the storage room."

I followed her out of the kitchen, down the creaking hall, through a barn-like structure, and into the yard. To my surprise, there were six other small stone buildings on the property. A tall black tank stood next to the building with the green door. I supposed it was a water tank and that the building was someone's house.

"That's David's house," said Joyce, as if reading my thoughts. "He is the caretaker for the property. He and his family live there."

A cow was tethered to a tree stump and six or eight chickens wandered around out front. A sheep wandered under the trees and rabbits bounced around beneath the clothesline. Shirts and socks and pants of all colors and sizes swayed in the wind.

In the distance, beyond the buildings, the mountains rose up into the sky. I took a deep breath, only to remember that our altitude was eight thousand feet. We were in the mountains. High, high in the mountains. Breathing would take some getting used to.

I followed Joyce along a little dirt path to the largest of the stone structures. The first three doors opened into classrooms full of desks with lessons written on chalkboards and children raising their hands in response to teacher's questions. The fourth door led to a room full of shelves, tables, clothes, school supplies, and toys. The smiley-face boxes had been placed in a mini-mound in the center of the space.

"You brought all this with you?" Joyce gawked.

"Yeah. My friends were excited to help," I said proudly.

"Is it a church? What people are so generous?" She looked confused.

"Nope. Just my friends." I chuckled to myself, thinking that my little furniture community in Albany had made a bigger impact than they knew.

"God Bless you!" Joyce beamed. "And all your friends."

There she was talking about God again. Openly. *Yikes.*

As we emptied the boxes, packages of socks, underwear, and T-shirts became the topic of conversation.

"White?" she asked, surprised.

I was surprised that she was surprised.

"White is so hard to keep clean." She shook her head, and a little piece of me started to understand.

I remembered the road leading to the house—two trenches of mud. White was simply not practical. I obviously hadn't done enough research.

We sorted boxes and bags, and made thirteen piles, one for each child who lived at the house. Pants, shirts, sweaters, underwear, socks, hats… and a toy or craft project for each child.

"So, where is your family?" I asked Joyce.

Joyce's deep dark brown eyes met mine. "Sylvester and I live with my parents. We live in town. Do you think he could have a new pair of pants?"

"Of course, he can have new pants! What else does he need?" Her smile made the room brighter as we added a pile for Sylvester.

In that small dark storage room, I also learned there was a third matron, Rebecca. Rebecca lived four hours to the east. She stayed at Hilltop Children's Home for three weeks out of the month and returned to her family for the fourth week. She was a single mom with four kids and would be back to work on Monday. Her kids would probably benefit from new socks or shoes, as well.

As we picked through dresses, skirts, jackets, school supplies, and T-shirts, I quickly came to realize that what I'd thought would be for thirteen kids would eventually turn out to help so many more.

When school let out, the day scholars who lived on the other side of town were piled into the Land Rover and transported home. The Hilltop Children's Home kids began their normal afternoon activities: doing homework, washing socks, and playing games. They kicked around the soccer ball and hung out in the sitting room with books, cards, and scraps of paper being folding into paper airplanes. The facility had its own pace, and gradually I would start to fall into it.

Each interaction revealed more to me. Conversations with the young Americans led me to realize that everyone was a volunteer—even Susan, the Country Director. She was there because, as she put it, "It was the right thing to do." I just wasn't sure how she was going to stay there for a year. A year! I was just hoping to get through another day. Yet, here she was, engrossed in the culture, having meetings in Nairobi and advocating for the children in this home. There was a powerhouse of a soul buried in this twenty-six-year-old woman.

Bruce's tenure was for six months—his main focus being community development. His intention was to help bring resources to the town as well as establish sustainable programs that would assist individuals in starting businesses or channeling energy into creating awareness about larger issues such as education, healthcare, and agriculture. These "kids"—as so many people back home might have referred to them—weren't getting paid. Their compassion and willingness to help reaped greater rewards than money.

But I was only just beginning to learn this.

At six o'clock, the children were called to the kitchen for dinner. A line was created that went out the door as Charlotte, Josh, Ava, Billy, and every other child bent to pick up a metal bowl full of rice and lentils off the floor. They smiled at Joyce and Phoebe and said "Thank You." Each of them found a spot at the long kitchen table, waited for everyone to arrive, bowed their heads, and then in unison said, "Father, we thank you for the supper. God, remember those who don't have any. In Jesus' name, we pray. Amen."

Did my ears just hear that? Did these kids just pray for people who have less than them?

The room was alive with activity, and conversations flew around the table. Thirteen self-assured, clean, animated small faces were quickly making heaps of food disappear. Laughter and chatter filled the air. The placemats were laminated maps of the world, and as Bruce threw out the question, "Where is England?" excitement erupted from the room. Some raised their hands, others yelled and pointed to the yellow island, and one small girl looked in bewilderment at her neighbor.

"Lynn, will you please explain to Helen what we are doing?" Bruce called out, noticing her confusion, as well.

Six-year-old, three-foot-high Lynn slipped into a conversation in a different language and pointed to the map. Helen's eyes lit up. She nodded and smiled.

"Helen is brand new to our home," Bruce later explained to me. "She was living in the bush with her grandmother and only understands the tribal language, Kikuyu."

"Kikuyu?" I asked. "I thought the native language was Swahili."

"Swahilli is the national language. Each tribe also has their own dialect, so most of our kids are tri-lingual. They help each other."

Tri-lingual? I shook my head in awe.

After dinner, the plates were cleared, the floors were swept, and the table was washed down. The whole group reconvened in the sitting room, five kids to a loveseat, two to a chair, and the rest sprawled on the dark wooden floor. Susan stood in front of the crowd and the nightly meeting commenced.

"How was school? Is everyone's homework done?"

There came a mixed response from the masses, and directions were passed out regarding who needed to continue their studies and spend more time on math or English or social studies. The older kids were designated to tutor the younger children with their work.

"When homework is done, we can watch a movie. Okay?"

Thirteen smiling, giggling children nodded their heads and dispersed throughout the house to study.

The sun had set during dinner, and at the same time a low roar rattled in the distance. Lights flashed on. The generator had been started. It was six-thirty at night. For some reason, I had assumed it would stay lighter later in the evening; *assumed* being the key word.

An hour later, kids were dressed in pajamas and cuddled into pillows and blankets on the floor. A fire was lit in the stone fireplace and the lights were turned off. Susan presented a black plastic sleeve full of DVDs and the overwhelming request was *High School Musical*.

I found a spot on the floor next to Ava, slouched down under the blanket, and settled in for the film. The nine-year-old kewpie doll cuddled in next to me and linked her tiny fingers with mine. My heart skipped a beat. *I am in Kenya, and yet, this feels a lot like family time when I was growing up. And there is a nine-year-old holding my hand.*

Thursday, May 6, 2010

On Tuesday, I assumed I would never leave the Hilltop Children's Home compound. Everything else beyond the complex was scary. Everyone was black—not brown, but black. Dark black. And there I was, a pale, blue-eyed blonde. There was no way of hiding it, no way of blending in. I was one of four white people in the town.

Then, today, only two days later, I woke up with the sudden urge to explore. I was in Kenya, and I simply couldn't spend my whole time there hiding out in the compound of the Hilltop Children's Home. I jumped out of bed excited for another day and decided that I would go into town.

But first, I had to prepare for going out. I needed to shower. After four or five days of using only Wet Ones, I had started to smell.

The volunteer bathroom had a regular tub in it, minus the shower curtain. There were knobs for both hot and cold water, but the water coming out of the faucet was distinctly cold, no matter what. A big black plastic bag with a yellow Sun Shower logo on it hung on a nail above the tub. *This* was the shower. *Maybe I don't smell that bad.* I lifted up my arm and sniffed, and then gagged. *Okay, maybe I do.*

Okay. Breathe. First things first, I went to the kitchen, found the pliers, and turned on the propane tank. I then lit the stove and waited patiently for the water to boil. The steaming water was then carried into the bathroom and poured into the two-inch opening of the black plastic bag. Cold water was added from the faucet, and I did a quick prayer hoping to get something close to warm. I climbed up on the edge of the tub, steadying myself with the sink, and hung the makeshift shower on the nail head.

Eventually, lukewarm water dribbled out from the end of the hose over my hair and body, and I made a mental note to allow lots of time for ordinary tasks. I also made another mental note—to buy more Wet Ones.

Around noon, Bruce, my new guardian angel, and I headed into town. The dirt road was full of ruts, troughs, and mud puddles. It was a mile trek past cow fields, chickens, and donkeys. Not exactly the wildlife I had expected in Kenya. What about the monkeys and the elephants and the zebras?

"Oh no, that's on safari. But maybe, just maybe, if we go to the forest, we'll see monkeys. And, oh yeah, that's Elephant Mountain in our backyard. Sometimes elephants hang out there. We usually know it because they step on the water pipes and we lose water," Bruce said nonchalantly.

Really? Elephants step on the pipes and you lose water?

On our way down the hill, masses of children on their way home from school yelled, "Mzungu," as they surrounded us.

"What does that mean?" I asked.

"White person. *Mzungu* means white person," Bruce laughed as he made an attempt to have a conversation with the little ones.

They smiled and giggled and bumped fists with the six-foot-tall white man, and then, instead of heading in their original direction, they turned and followed us down the hill. It was as if Bruce was the Pied Piper and these kids were happy to just walk along with him.

I didn't quite understand what was going on.

Why are they following us? What's the big deal?

When I lost my footing in the mud traps, one of the small boys reached out his hand and saved me from becoming a mud-drenched disaster. His big brown eyes looked up at me, we shared a smile, and then he timidly wove his fingers between mine. Our hands stayed clasped together and we walked on in silence, smirking at each other.

Then, there we were, the whole group of us, smack dab in the middle of Naivasha-town. The road changed from dirt and mud to tarmac and dirt. Bruce sent the children away with, "Go home. Go home." He knew they needed to head back to their families and the duties of the day.

Donkeys and sheep were lying on the side of the roads. A group of motorbike drivers sat on a concrete platform waiting for their next fares.

"Mzungu, mzungu!" They waved their hands, pointing to their bikes. Bruce and I were the only white people on the street, so they must have been talking to us. Bruce waved back a "no thank you" and they went back to their conversations.

My heart was beating in my throat. My eyes darted in every direction, very aware of my surroundings and on heightened alert. I felt like I had just landed on a different planet. Sensors were buzzing throughout my body. *One step in front of the other.* Bruce had been there for a few weeks and he seemed to know exactly what he was doing.

Just follow him.

Shops lined both sides of the dusty thoroughfare. The KCB bank was to the left, the blue Supa Duka shop on the right. There were green Safaricom logos, yellow Kodak emblems, and a sign for Wisdom Café, the local internet café. A two-story, yellow concrete building had the Tusker Lager emblem painted on the front. The Gimwa Hotel sign swung from the overhang in front of the local diner. Shop after shop touted their wares: clothes, school supplies, cakes, and tea. Motorbikes whizzed by and buses full of people beeped as they passed us. The horns weren't the friendly kind. They were the "get out of the way" kind. Pedestrians obviously did not have the right of way.

"Be careful walking on the streets," Bruce said. "They're aggressive drivers."

An alley cut through two battered shops and opened into an outdoor market, full of rows of kiosks neatly crafted from raw lumber and used tarps. Within each booth, a woman sat behind her produce: bananas, mangos, avocados, pineapples, watermelon, potatoes, rice, and beans. Bruce approached the attractive, middle-aged woman in the first booth on the right.

"Jambo," he said as he nodded and picked up seven bananas.

"Jambo sana," she replied.

"How much for each banana?"

"Five shillings." The strong accent suggested this might be the only English this sturdy, hard-working woman knew.

He pulled coins out of his pocket and paid the woman thirty-five shillings.

"How much is that?" I asked, wondering about the conversion rate from dollars to shillings.

"About thirty cents. But I'm not sure if I overpaid or not. They'll always try to overcharge us because we're white. I have to figure out the right price for bananas soon," he said. "It's a game."

I was forewarned. But, thirty cents? He was going to negotiate over thirty cents? This seemed absurd.

Our next stop was at the pharmacist, otherwise known as the chemist.

"Jambo," Bruce cheerfully greeted the young man standing behind the counter at the small wooden shop.

"Jambo sana," replied the shop owner as they shook hands.

"I need some eyedrops for my eyes, please."

The owner turned to the fully stocked, handmade wooden shelves behind him and found a small box that resembled Visine.

"Will this help?" he asked with a British accent.

"This is perfect. Asante sana." Bruce smiled.

The negotiation process started regarding the price. *Wow, everything gets negotiated. My mother and her garage sale haggling would do well here.* Eventually, the sale price was agreed upon. Sixty cents. The shop keeper wrapped the product neatly into paper and the exchange was complete.

We bid farewell with a smile after a fair negotiation and headed home. I wanted to ask my new friend Bruce about all the dickering, but my breathing was labored and it was difficult to speak while walking. I felt out of shape and embarrassed.

"It's the altitude," Bruce chuckled, noticing my panting. "It'll take a few days to get used to it, but don't worry, you'll be fine."

Yeah, yeah, I'll be fine. Someday, I will be able to breathe again. And someday I won't be terrified to talk to people on the street. Yeah, yeah, someday this will all make sense and I will be fine.

God, I hoped so.

Cutie Bruce picked up the slack and brought me up to speed on who he was and where he came from. He had no difficulty breathing as he chatted about his family and his hometown of Spokane, Washington. Bruce's family ran a successful insurance business, which he'd been a part of for a few years after college.

"The company was getting ready to expand and I had to commit one way or another—was I going to do insurance my whole life or was I supposed to try something different?"

My feet were trudging uphill through muddy ruts and my head was nodding up and down as I wheezed, "I know that feeling."

"I wanted to see other parts of the world. I wanted to do something meaningful."

I was so glad to hear someone else say the words that had run through my head for so long. I wasn't alone.

I *was* huffing and puffing. And muddy and dirty and a little stinky. But I was content.

Finally, we reached the wooden gate and made our way into the Hilltop Children's Home compound. The kids were out of school and we were once again enveloped with little ones hugging and screaming, "Uncle Bruce! Uncle Bruce, watch me! Watch me!" The gentle twenty-five-year-old soul beamed as he threw Helen over his shoulder and patted young Billy on the back.

Kids. Kids. Everywhere. Love flew around as fast and free as the soccer ball in the air.

Later that night, after homework, dinner, and TV time, the generator was shut off and all the kids were tucked into bed. Instead of crawling into my bunkbed with the rest of the college students, I made my way outside and sat on the stone steps. Thousands of twinkling dots danced in the blacker than black sky. As I thought about home, about cancer, about Crack, about furniture, about my friends, and about life on the other side of the world, the smell of the fire coming from the house put me at ease. The sound of barking dogs in the distance added a touch of normality. The cool fresh air touched my skin, and I took a deep breath and let the wave of life rush over me. This wasn't so bad. I was learning how to breathe again.

Saturday, May 8, 2010

Getting used to living in a house of thirteen kids didn't take as long as I would have thought. It reminded me of my childhood—our house had always been the hub…. Friends were always coming in and out of the house, stopping in to say hi, playing cards with my mom, and getting ready for school plays or Christmas fundraisers. My childhood was active and loud and full of laughter and love—much like this house in Naivasha. Occasionally, there were fights about who'd had the Matchbox car first or who got to use the iPod or who got to be playing with the hulahoop (a.k.a. old bicycle tire), but all in all, it was pretty normal. Just a bunch of kids growing up in the same house, sharing their stuff.

Saturday was typically laundry day for volunteers.

Lynn watched me curiously with my pile of clothes. This young lady was a bit intimidating.

"Call me Lynn Obama," she announced with a strong voice.

Well, this was interesting, I thought. "Why's that?" I asked.

"I'm going to be the first woman President of Kenya. NOT the first lady. FIRST WOMAN PRESIDENT." Determination and drive were exuded from this little girl, and her missing front teeth and tightly braided hair only added to her allure.

"Auntie, do you want me to help? Can I teach you?"

"Yes, please," I responded with what must have been an obvious look of confusion and admiration on my face.

"We need a bucket!" Her voice rang strong as I obediently followed her into the hallway in search of a receptacle to be used for this clothes-washing experience. "Now we need hot water." She marched towards the "down" kitchen, the second kitchen located at the far end of the house, outside the main living structure. It was a stone enclosure with a metal roof and three wood-fired burners. A huge pot of water was boiling on the stove. Lynn skillfully took the plastic bucket sitting nearby and dunked it into the pot of hot water.

"Whoa, whoa, let me get that," I said to her.

"Auntie, Auntie, it's good. I can do this."

"No, no. I'll get the bucket." The last thing I wanted was a six-year-old getting third degree burns trying to carry a bucket of water for my laundry.

We made our way back to the tree stump and hoisted the bucket on top. Another volunteer had suggested that it was easier to bend over the bucket on the stump than to reach all the way down to the ground—surely saying something about getting older and how long I would actually be bent over scrubbing away at these clothes.

Lynn added the powered soap and then, piece-by-piece, we scrubbed each shirt, pair of pants, and sock. Lynn's system was far superior to mine. She would add soap, scrub out any stains, ring out the soap, and place the piece on a towel on the ground. She scrubbed about ten items to my one.

"See, Auntie, like this." Her tiny hands moved quickly back and forth, removing the mud caked on the bottom of my pant legs.

Yeah, Lynn, I see what you are doing, but I don't get it. My knuckles are bleeding and my fingers hurt and I can't get any of the dirt out!

I was such a pansy ass.

Within an hour, the dirty pile was gone. Lynn smiled and said, "Now we rinse them and do it again!" *What? Again? I didn't really care how clean my clothes were at this point. As long as I didn't smell too bad, that was fine with me.* But, no... Lynn was excited about this second washing—excited to get the dirt out of the clothes.

She obviously had much more patience than I did.

As we finished our pile of laundry, hung it all on the line to dry, and made our way into the house, Heather passed by.

"Hey, just FYI... Ester comes to the house every day to do laundry. She's always looking for extra work and the money to go with it."

I needed some Neosporin or something for my bloody knuckles.

"How much does she charge?" I asked.

"I give her 500 shillings for a bag full of clothes."

The conversions were running through my head. This was something close to five dollars. I couldn't wait to meet Ester, and there was no way that I would be negotiating that price. I might even pay her extra.

Later that afternoon, I relaxed in the sitting room with a book and a kid, recovering from the grueling laundry experience. Susan passed through the room, and stopped and smiled.

"How's it going?" she asked.

"Well, I'm learning," I sighed as I gave Adam a little hug.

"It will all come together. Just hang in there," she assured me.

I was starting to believe the words of these so-called "kids" who were actually running this organization. After all, I didn't have many options.

"We would really like to clean out one of the other storage rooms to use as space for donations. Would you be willing to take on that project?"

"Yup. Whatever you want." I was happy to help in some way.

"Let's go check out the space."

Alex, Susan, and I made our way across the yard to the stone structure with all the four green doors. Susan put the old-fashioned key in the lock and wiggled the mechanism until the door opened. There was a thick layer of dirt covering the concrete floor and the dust whipped up with the movement of the door. A small choke escaped my throat.

"It needs to be swept and mopped." Susan smiled as she handed me the broom—a bunch of dried stalks tied tightly together. It resembled something similar to a corn husk that I would have hung on my front door during Thanksgiving at home.

Shit. Here we go again. Nothing is as easy as it seems here.

Susan laughed as our eyes met. Yeah, I would learn. She headed off in one direction and I headed off to find the blue bucket that I'd used earlier to wash my clothes. I stopped at the spigot, filled it with cold water, and made my way back to the fifteen-by-fifteen dusty, dirty space.

Before long, Lynn was standing in the doorway assessing the situation. She shook her head, left the building, and returned with another broom in hand. The little powerhouse bent over at the waist and made quick movements with her wrist, easily sweeping the dirt out the door with this peculiar tool. As the cloud of dust dissipated, she poured the water from the bucket all over the floor.

Oh my, I thought, *I hope she knows what she's doing.* It seemed like a big mud pie on the floor. Broom in hand, she swept the water out bit-by-bit, out the door. I followed her lead. Before I knew it, our floor was clean—a relative description while in the hills of Kenya.

Lynn was an impressive teacher, undoubtedly capable beyond her years. She would make an amazing President, and I was very aware that I was a student in this distant land.

After dinner that evening, Joyce and Rebecca, who had returned from her week at home, helped to distribute the new clothes. One at a time, the children were brought into the sitting room. New pants, shoes, dresses, tops, jackets, underwear, pajamas, toys, books, and educational games were all part of each child's goodie pile. One by one, each child sat next to me and said, "Thank you! Thank you, Auntie!"

"My friends in America sent these to you. They have been thinking of you and wanted to send you special presents. Lynn Obama smiled widely and held up the picture of a little red-headed girl that had been included in her letter, and said, "This is my new friend Taylor, and I love her."

I had no idea how I would ever express this feeling of gratitude to the people who had been so generous. Words would never suffice.

After each child received their gifts, there was a fashion show. They tried on their clothes, swapped items when necessary based on sizes, and paraded through the sitting room proud as peacocks. One after another, children beamed gleefully because of their new socks, pajamas, or dress. Eight-year-old Billy entered the room wearing a light blue oxford shirt, tan khakis, a navy blue tie, and a black belt. He stood tall and made sure the buttons on his cuffs were done.

"Billy, Billy, look here," I said as I snapped a picture and captured the moment for myself.

"Now, go put your new clothes away, change into your pajamas, and get ready for bed," Auntie Joyce said.

"Tomorrow, you will clean your closets and take out things you no longer wear."

Susan later explained that the children donated their old clothes. When they received new items, they would take the old and bring them to other children in the community who were in need. Giving to those less fortunate. The lesson of community service was being embedded in their young brains. They were being taught kindness and compassion.

After everyone was in bed, Joyce came and sat next to me in the sitting room.

"Auntie?"

I burst out into a wide smile. I loved Joyce. She was quickly becoming one of my Kenyan sisters.

"Joyce?"

"Auntie, I went to help Billy get ready for bed and put his clothes away. He asked me about the tags. He wanted to know if he could keep them. You see, he's never had anything new before. I told him he could definitely keep the tags. He put them in his box for safe-keeping."

It was another one of those moments, the ones where my heart broke open a little more.

Monday, May 10, 2010

After one full week in Naivasha, I truly believed that my goal to drop my extra fifteen chemo pounds was not an unreasonable expectation. The diet of rice and beans couldn't possibly be that fattening. Eggs and toast in the morning was a meal low in calories. Fresh fruit was abundant. There were lots of carbs and not a whole lot of protein, but mile after mile of going back and forth to town would burn those calories. The sweet Kenyan tea, however, would most likely be the death of me. I could drink it by the boatload.

Saturday morning was Bruce's standing committee meeting regarding the upcoming Day of the African Child event, and I decided to tag along to check it out.

"What is this thing about anyway?" I asked Bruce while we walked to town. I didn't wheeze as much as I had a few days earlier.

"It's a tribute to honor the kids of Soweto."

"Soweto?" I felt dumb.

"It's in South Africa. In 1976, nearly ten thousand African children launched a peaceful protest about the inferior quality of their education. They wanted to be taught in their native language and wanted resources to be equally distributed between blacks and whites. As the march reached critical mass at a police blockade, police fired on the crowds, unprovoked. Hundreds of young boys and girls were shot down, and in the two weeks of protest that followed, hundreds more were killed or injured. June 16th has become a continental day of memorial."

"Oh shit. Kids were killed because they wanted a better education?"

"Yup. Since 1991, there has been a movement towards remembrance of this event. It matches our mission—giving children the education and support they need to thrive in this changing world. And what better way to promote these ideals than having a party?" He smiled.

I was totally on board. I loved parties.

The planning committee gathered at the Gimwa Diner and consisted of local businessmen, some NGO workers, and various government employees. Bruce introduced me to the team as we sat down and ordered tea. It was the same as planning any gala back home, except our lunch consisted of rice and beans, and there were chickens and sheep wandering around in the street outside the window.

The total budget for the event would not exceed two thousand dollars. The intent was to involve the entire community in a parade that would lead from the Gimwa area all the way to the "other side," and unveil the new Hilltop Children's Home School that was nearing completion. At the site, we would host a party complete with music, dancing, and speeches from politicians aimed at promoting the importance of education. Estimated attendance was two thousand children plus their families. Normal logistics needed to be addressed: police involvement, audio systems, marketing, and decorations.

Bruce began the dispensing of tasks.

"Louis, can you coordinate the details of the police and make sure that all the schools are ready to submit poems for the poetry contest? Peter, can you work with the radio station and make sure they have all the equipment they need? We will use the roof of the school as the stage and will need to make sure the speakers and the amps and the electricity are all accounted for. Jimmie Gait will have all his own equipment, so we will need to coordinate with his staff, as well." Jimmie Gait was the Kenyan version of Justin Timberlake.

"We will need a tent for the dignitaries. Martha Karua is coming. We will need to serve them lunch during the event." Martha Karua was one of the 2012 Presidential nominees.

National political figures. Pop stars. A lot of kids. All on a hill in Naivasha.

Amazing.

After the meeting, I stood on the side of the road with a few of the kids from Hilltop Children's Home who had appeared from out of nowhere. Lots of other local children came by, staring at my white skin and wanting to touch the baby-fine new hair that was sprouting out of my head. One child in particular was very bold. He knew the words "give me" as well as other words such as *bag*, *watch*, and *money*. In no way did I want to condone begging, though. That was not why I was there.

Sternly, I addressed the bold boy and said, "No, that's rude."

I didn't know if he understood English, but I was certain he understood my tone. These kids knew what they were doing. They were smart and wanted more for themselves. I couldn't blame them for asking, but it seemed like a fine line between asking for help and asking for a handout. Sometimes I wondered what the real difference was.

Thursday, May 13, 2010

The days have started to whisk by. Monday morning, I became a tutor for three children. My task is to spend time with them—one on one. *And then what?* I wondered. What was I supposed to do with these kids? I had zero teaching skills. My life revolved around chairs and desks and conference tables.

But no one seemed to care. My schedule was assigned.

8:30 – Helen
9:15 – David
11:00 – Paul

At eight-thirty, Helen stood in the doorway with her head hung low, looking at the floor. I knelt down and looked in her face.

"Hi, Helen." Her big brown eyes stared back at me. "Should we get a book?"

Her head tilted around a bit and there was a brief moment of eye contact followed by a slight nod. We made our way to the bookshelf, where she fingered the stacks, pulled out a hardcover publication showcasing animals, and sheepishly handed it to me. We held hands and headed down the hall to the blue upholstered sofa in the sitting room. We sat side by side and I pulled Helen close as she opened the book.

"Should we read together?" I asked.

She stared at me, her facial expression illegible.

"Okay, well, I'll just read for now," I said.

As I read, she stared at the pictures, quiet as a mouse.

"Do you like penguins? Do you know what these are? They're birds that live where it's really cold? Yeah. That's ice and snow in the picture," I said, pointing to the black and white walking bird.

She stared at me. I smiled back at her. She didn't say a word.

I am the worst tutor ever. What the hell am I supposed to do? What am I doing here? These were the thoughts that flew like wildfire through my brain. When one book was done, the teeny-tiny little girl with tight braids in her hair quietly returned it to the bookcase and then came back to me with another picture book about fruits and vegetables. She cuddled into my side as we turned the pages one at a time, looking at oranges and mangos and corn on the cob and carrots, her big brown eyes intense and focused. I hugged her close.

At nine-fifteen, David arrived and spoke to Helen in their language. She smiled at me and left the room. David's devilish grin engulfed his round, cheerful face.

"Helen doesn't speak English yet."

Well then, THAT explains everything.

David was nine, and one of the first children who had come to live in Hilltop Children's Home. He was being tutored to improve his reading skills, although he spoke English very well.

"What language did you just talk to Helen in?" I asked.

"Kikuyu," David replied. "She just got here. She doesn't know Swahili yet."

David joyfully headed down the hall to select reading material, and returned with Dr. Seuss's *Oh, the Places You'll Go!* We flew through the pages, taking turns reading the limericks aloud. The colorful drawings and rhythmic words delivered a meaningful message. *Take life by storm. Don't wait. Move mountains. Don't take no for an answer.*

This was powerful stuff to read to an orphan in Kenya. Actually, it was powerful stuff to read to a forty-two-year-old American woman, too.

Afterwards, he went for another book. We sounded out words together, talked about silent letters, and read about *The Cat in the Hat*. He was an animated kid with eyes that shone bright. He was thrilled to sit on a sofa and read with an adult—someone who paid attention to only him.

Porridge break meant that school let out, and seventy kids burst into the yard creating a spontaneous eruption of energy. I guess that's what kids do at recess.... Burn off energy. One by one, the kids formed a line at the "down" kitchen and were handed a blue plastic cup with the word OK printed on it. Porridge was their mid-morning snack, a gloppy blend of flour, water, and chocolate powder. One of the older girl students, Dorothy, asked if I wanted to try hers. I tried not to crinkle my nose when I replied, "Oh, no. That's so sweet of you. It's your snack. You eat it."

Dorothy smiled as she asked, "Where are you from?"

"America."

"Oh, America. Obama!" another girl shouted excitedly.

"Yes. Obama. Do you like him?"

"We love Obama. He is Kenyan, you know?"

This coming from a ten-year-old. These were some smart kids.

Break ended and my next student arrived at the door—Paul. Small, thin, beautiful Paul with the torn and tattered shoes. This child was one of the fifty day scholars transported daily from the "other side" of town to attend school at the Hilltop Children's Home facility.

I extended my hand and bent over to introduce myself. His slight face looked to the ground. I had learned my lesson with Helen. Paul probably didn't speak any English.

Gently, I took the boy's hand and led him into the playroom to stand in front of the bookshelf. He was in awe. I don't think he had set foot inside the stone house before. His timid eyes looked from me to the bookcase, then to the stack of stuffed animals and racks of toys. I got down on my knees and rubbed his back while directing his attention to the colorful spines neatly organized on the wooden bookcase.

"Let's pick a book together," I whispered.

He looked at me and stared. Maybe I scared him because I was white. "Should we read this one?"

No response. My words weren't registering.

"Okay. We'll read this." My fingers held a small red paperback with hand-drawn pictures of dogs and cats and simple words. I nodded and led him down the hallway to the room with the blue sofa.

Paul stood in the doorway and scanned the space which had a fireplace and a TV and a sofa and two chairs. I patted the soft cushion next to me. Cautiously, he took a seat on the sofa, making sure to keep lots of space between us.

I flipped the pages and read aloud about Dick and Jane and the dog and the cats.

I pointed to the picture of the dog. "Dog."

And then the cat. "Cat."

Paul stared silently at the picture, with his hands neatly folded in his lap. For half an hour, we went through book after book from opposite ends of the three-seat sofa. I flipped pages and read words and smiled at him. I think I actually broke out in a sweat, my nervousness escaping through my pores.

When our session ended, Paul silently went back out to the yard. I retreated to the bottom bunk, feeling lousy and full of angst. I had no idea how to do this. I wasn't a teacher. I wasn't even a mother.

Mental exhaustion was kicking in. I wasn't capable of making a difference. The problems were too big.

Wednesday, May 19, 2010

At forty-three years old, I was the oldest person at the home. Inspiration came on a daily basis by watching people half my age CHOOSE to be of service to those in need. It wasn't a religious mission but maybe it was a spiritual quest. It was an acute awareness of humanitarian suffering and need. There may also have been some egoism involved, thinking that "we" knew best. It was a fine line.

College-aged volunteers were showing up on a regular basis, settling in to this minimalist lifestyle, full of excitement, adventure, and open hearts. They were taking on the world, wanting to make it a better place, and their enthusiasm was contagious. In the meantime, I was getting a new nineteen-year-old roommate in my dorm.

A few days ago, Susan and I headed to Nairobi to pick up Olivia, an African Studies major from UVM who arrived in the middle of the night. Travel back to Naivasha would not be safe at one o'clock in the morning, so we made arrangements to stay at the Terminal Hotel in Nairobi. At twelve dollars a night, I had to wrap my head around the fact that you got what you paid for.

Dirty mosquito nets were tied in knots hanging from the ceiling. Seedy, blue chenille bedspreads covered two twin beds, but fortunately the linens appeared clean and the pillowcases were definitely white. The small, dingy white sink and pitted mirror hung on a wall in the sleeping area. The toilet and shower were in a small room behind a rather warped wooden door. A small desk and chair finished off the layout of the room. Fluorescent lightbulbs buzzed overhead. The upside? There was a power outlet for us to plug our phones in. And it worked all night long—without a generator.

I didn't see any little beetles running around, but my guess was that was only because the lights were on. A rowdy, raucous bar directly beneath us completed the experience. *Man, I'm too old for this. Tell me again, why didn't I just take a trip to the Caribbean?* Luckily, I had packed the Ambien left over from my chemo days. I popped a pill and waited for the effect to kick in as the music blared from below and visions of cockroaches crawling all over me ran through my brain. It was going to be one of those nights.

The hours dragged on and eventually the morning arrived. Blonde-haired, blue-eyed Olivia and I headed to Naivasha while Susan stayed behind to attend meetings in the city. My assignment for the day was to get Olivia settled into life at Hilltop Children's Home. We had hired Kenneth, the driver, to bring us back to the house. It was the same trip I had made the week before, but for some reason, this time the smells and the crazy reckless driving ate at every little piece of me. Maybe it was the left-over Ambien or the lack of a good cup of coffee. As Kenneth drove us through the windy, bumpy, muddy roads, swerving incessantly to miss pot holes, I tried to put Olivia at ease. My stomach definitely wasn't on the same page. Minute by minute, I felt my insides gurgling as I pointed out the Great Rift Valley and the scenery along the way, trying to establish myself as a reputable tour guide.

As I turned blue in the face, Olivia asked, "Are you okay?"

I pushed my hand to my mouth and feverishly shook my head *NO* while gesturing to the driver to pull over. I threw the door open, leaned out, and left the insides of my stomach on the muddy road beneath me. Then I gracefully wiped my mouth and closed the door.

I smiled a pleasant smile, looked at Olivia, and said, "Sorry about that. Let's go home." I wish I had been more graceful with the "Welcome to Hilltop Children's Home" task. More like Bruce with his hand-written note and calla lily on the front. But, nope. My version was a bit different.

Poor Olivia. I did my best.

Days later, Susan, Peter—a Kenyan advocate for Hilltop Children's Home—and I walked into town. Peter was a handsome man, neatly dressed with sparkling white teeth. He was part of an organization called Shining Stars, which was dedicated to helping people in the community that were house-bound. He did service work for those dying at home of AIDS and other diseases, often delivering food and supplies to people who couldn't move.

At the bottom of the hill, we found eleven-year-old Regina standing on the side of the road staring out at the green field. She was dressed in her navy blue school uniform, but her feet were bare and sinking into the ground. Her ankles and calves were caked in mud.

"Why isn't she in school?" Susan asked Peter.

Peter turned to Regina and had a short conversation in what I thought was Swahili. Regina's blank expression didn't reveal much.

"She doesn't have shoes and they won't let her in," Peter explained.

Susan quickly filled me in. Regina had epilepsy, and had been married off at only ten years old. The chief later removed her from that abusive relationship and put her in the custody of another relative. Her new guardian obviously couldn't afford shoes for the child.

Raindrops drizzled down from the sky while the four of us stood in the middle of the road, which was gradually turning into a mud pit. Regina stared blankly at the adults surrounding her.

"Please take her home to her guardian. She shouldn't be out here in the rain," Susan told Peter as she departed for her meeting with one of the local officials. I remained with Peter and Regina.

Naivasha was a small town, and it seemed as though everyone was familiar with Regina's story. She would be taken back to her guardian and the same thing would happen again tomorrow.

"How much are shoes?" I asked out loud as I walked next to Peter and Regina.

"Three hundred shillings," he replied.

I calculated the exchange in my head. *Two dollars and seventy-five cents.*

"Can you help me go to the market and buy her a pair?" I asked.

With Regina in tow, we headed through the alley to the open space full of vendors. Past the produce kiosks, we found a large blue tarp on the ground, covered with rain boots of all shapes and sizes. Regina picked up a pair and looked at me. I nodded my head and smiled. She tried on different sizes and colors, and ended up with a rainbow pair of rubber, knee-high boots. Peter went through the obligatory negotiation process with the vendor and I paid the elderly woman three hundred shillings.

We then made our way to the kiosk selling socks, and Peter started the bargaining process again. I paid forty-two shillings—fifty cents—for a pair of long, grey nylon socks with blue stripes, and handed them to Regina. She sat on the ground, pulled the socks onto her muddy feet, and slipped them into her new boots. She stood up and didn't say a word. As I took her hand in mine, she looked up and smiled.

Our next stop was the produce stand, and the negotiation process started all over again. Peter argued back and forth with the man in order to get three bananas for five cents each, which I promptly handed to Regina.

"Let's go have tea," Peter then suggested. I was quick to say yes. I wanted to learn more about him and his group.

The three of us made our way out of the market, down the street, and into the Gimwa Diner. We ordered tea and mandazi, which reminded me of donuts. As we ate, Peter and I talked about our lives, which seemed so different and yet in some ways were so alike. Regina sat next to me, eating her mandazi eagerly. Afterwards, she got up and left without a word.

Peter and I eventually parted ways and I headed back up the hill to the compound. Lost in my emotions, I couldn't help but think that there were many other children living in circumstances similar to Regina's in the immediate vicinity. I wanted to go buy a hundred pair of rainboots to hand out to kids. I wanted to do something big. But what about the next hundred children? And the hundred children after that? And what difference did rainboots really make? They would eventually wear out or the children would outgrow them. The soles would be torn and mud would still get caked onto their feet.

I was being exposed to poverty. I saw the desperation and the hopelessness. And I wished I was reading about this in a book instead of actually walking through it.

Trudging along in the mud, I contemplated the meaning of my visit. *What was my goal? How could I help? Why was I there?* For the first two weeks, I'd dreamed that I could make a difference. Do more fundraising, send books and clothes, start a new farming program, help with the HIV/AIDS issues. It was humbling to realize that assisting three students in learning how to spell the word "cat" would have to be enough.

I spent the rest of the day getting better acquainted with my simple self.

The next day, Olivia and I trekked into town to purchase fruit, vegetables, and bread. Our walk home coincided with the end of the school day. Children from the area schools were wandering the streets of town, and as we started to head back up the hill, there was a parade of different-colored school uniforms following us. I never quiet understood how fascinated they were with us simply because we were white. Children looked at us with wonder and giggled when we engaged with them. The older ones wanted to touch us and maybe hold our hands. The even older ones wanted to practice their English with us. As I turned around to take stock of how many kids were part of this pack, I noticed Regina in the back of the group, wearing her new boots and a smile that went from ear to ear.

This was one of those moments when, even though my heart was bursting with joy, I thought about cutting my trip short. I was struck by the poverty and the dirt, by the tragic histories of most of these children, and by the pain. The other volunteers were totally capable of doing this work. Maybe I was just getting in the way. Maybe I should go home, sell some more chairs, and just send money.

But then reality would sink in. These kids had been left to die on the streets or in the woods. These kids came from places where there were three hundred children and one bathroom and barely any food. These kids knew about desperation and hopelessness. I wanted to hug them and love them all. I wanted to touch them. I wanted to read to them and hold their hands and somehow believe that their lives would eventually be better. I wanted to believe in the good of the world.

My interaction with Regina had fractured my belief system. I didn't know what I didn't know. It might be emotionally disturbing for me, but wasn't that the point? All I had to do was look around and realize that there was a bigger purpose. I still had work to do.

Tuesday, June 1, 2010

Bruce recently returned from safari and raved about the Ole-Moran Tented Camp in the Maasai Mara ecosystem. After listening to him gush about flat mattresses, hot running water, and buffet dinners, it became apparent that I was in need of a little break. Yes, after one month in this environment, I wanted to escape. I was privileged and able to check out of this life on a whim. Olivia and I talked about a trip, made some quick phone calls, did some negotiating, and, before we knew it, we were headed to the land of zebras and lions and warthogs.

Traveling within Kenya was an adventure in itself. Following multiple treacherous car rides, my college-aged traveling buddy and I let out a sigh of relief when we finally arrived at the safari company's office and put our feet on solid ground.

"That was like being on the fastest, craziest, most insane roller coaster EVER," Olivia whispered under her breath, obviously hoping not to offend the driver.

Olivia and I were first introduced to David, the safari guide. He was a thick, stocky man dressed in a green button-down shirt, khaki pants, and hiking boots.

"Welcome to the Ole Moran Tented Camp. We are so happy you are here." David shook our hands, smiled brightly, and placed our bags in the back of a safari green Land Rover.

"It's a five hour ride to the Mara. I hope you'll be happy with your African Massage," he said, snickering.

Olivia and I shot each other wary looks and loaded into the vehicle along with six other college-aged kids from Norway, Canada, and the United States. Young adults chatted about their work in birthing centers in Uganda, medical clinics in western Kenya, and graduate work at home associated with human rights. I pretended that the constant bumping and jolting along the well-worn road *was* actually coming from a masseuse and that somehow my back would feel better when this ride was complete. It wasn't easy. The road was a disaster, and long and never-ending.

But eventually David's sarcasm would become charming... eventually.

David educated us on Kenyan history as we headed down the escarpments into the flat of the Great Rift Valley. The paved road had been built in the 1940s by Italian prisoners of war being housed in the area. Mile by mile, these men constructed the main thoroughfare that connect the plains of the Mara and the Serengeti to points east, stretching roughly one hundred and fifty miles. Surprisingly, the project managers for these construction jobs were British women, placed here specifically because the government believed them to be honest rather than corrupt or prone to taking bribes, as had been the history with men. Now, I got the distinct impression that there'd not been that much maintenance done on these roads since they had been built—hence the the so-called African Massage.

Five hours later, we landed at our final destination and let out a whoop. A tent had never looked so good to me. After a long, hot shower and a four-course meal served in a lavish open-air dining room, we fell into bed, going quickly to sleep on the plains of the Maasai Mara.

For the next two days, my senses were inundated with the sights, sounds, and smells of nature at its best.

Saturday evening, we roamed the plains of East Africa in the green Land Rover with the top off. A short rain had passed through and the air was muggy and dense. The sun was setting and the sky was turning pink and orange. In the distance, David spotted a herd of water buffalo grazing on the plain. We made our way through windy grass trails and eventually parked within yards of hundreds of giant black animals with horns. None of the creatures even acknowledged our existence. They were obviously very comfortable with visitors. Kind of like Busch Gardens on steroids.

The group of us *oohed* and *awed* and snapped pictures just like any other group of tourists. Within minutes, however, one of the students from Norway whispered, "Lions," and pointed to two golden cats slithering along in the grass beside our truck. Their eyes were focused intently on a lone buffalo. David picked up his radio and spoke quickly into the receiver, giving notice to other safari companies about the activity.

Much to my surprise, thirty other Land Rovers, complete with international tourists and thousands of dollars' worth of camera equipment, arrived within minutes of the communication. White and green safari vehicles circled the herd of buffalo, the only sound in the air being the *click, click, click* of the cameras.

The lions immediately disappeared into the tall grasses, finding their optimal positions as the oblivious buffalo continued to eat its last meal.

In awe, we watched the episode unfold.

The lions strategically placed themselves between the buffalo and the herd. They waited and crawled and watched as their next meal chewed on the tall grasses. Eventually, an explosion of energy burst forth as the two massive cats attacked the tranquil creature. Sounds of agony and fear and tearing flesh and clicking cameras filled the air. Dust kicked up from the earth and the colors of black and gold and blood became a massive blur. Within seconds, it was over. Two lions were contently tearing apart the beastly buffalo as a hundred people snapped shots. It was the circle of life captured via digital camera. The pictures in *National Geographic* always looked so remote and desolate. I'd never imagined these shoots were really like paparazzi sightings.

The next day, we visited a Maasai village, complete with introductions to the chief and a trip to their market. I was overcome with a sense of sadness. These people were charging a "tour fee" for others to come and visit their homes. It felt obtrusive and bold and disrespectful. Yet, tourism was a source of income for these people. It was one more paradox of visiting Kenya.

David educated us on the Maasai lifestyle and the wildlife on the plains. During our rides, he gave us information on zebras and ostriches and giraffes. Warthogs and jackals and hyenas also made random appearances.

"The Maasai believe that God made the wildebeest with the leftovers of other animals: the head of a beast, the neck of a lion, the tail of a horse, the body of a buffalo, the tongue of a giraffe."

Quite a mishmash, but when I saw the odd creature up close, it made sense.

We learned that jackals acted as midwives and scavengers at the same time, that giraffes could develop high blood pressure due to their long necks, and that an elephant's gestation period is two years. Pen in hand, I wrote down every detail David shared with us, knowing I would never remember them all otherwise.

After two days of game drives, spectacular sunsets, and being witness to a majestic life on the plains of the Serengeti, I was missing home. There were only so many animals to gawk over. I was ready to get back to the kids in Naivasha.

Thursday, June 3, 2010

At Hilltop Children's Home, there was a tempo and routine that kept the place moving efficiently. Morning chores included sweeping and washing the floors, doing the dishes, and cleaning the bathrooms. After breakfast, there came tutoring in the morning, helping with projects in the afternoon, homework after school, dinner, family time, and bedtime stories.

Tutoring had taken on a life of its own. Helen began picking out different books and trying to sound out the words. She loved doing puzzles and playing Concentration with a deck of cards. I knew this wasn't what real teachers typically did with their students, but my mom had raised us playing cards. She'd said it was good for our math skills, so I figured it was okay. Helen would clap her hands when she found a pair and squeal, "Your turn!" when they didn't match. This was the beginning of her English vocabulary. Bizarre.

David's side project was writing a book titled *King David*. I helped him fold construction paper into little squares and then staple the edges shut. On the cover, he drew a picture of a little boy with a crown placed squarely on top of his head. Each page contained a different picture: airplanes, cows, houses, and trees. He wrote his story in different colored markers, constantly excited over his progress and always smiling from ear to ear with his face full of the cutest dimples ever.

I came to learn that David was the animal lover of the house. He regularly took the cow for walks and cared for Josie, the family dog. He built shelters for the rabbits and, on more than one occasion, he brought a baby chameleon or oversized grasshopper to our tutoring session.

Paul was the most challenging of the three kids I dealt with in tutoring. He often seemed uncomfortable around me and wasn't quite sure what to make of being in the house or around the books. He didn't seem to know how to act or what to say or do. After our first few sessions, I realized that he did in fact speak English; he was just very shy. I asked him questions to try to coax him out of his shell, but oftentimes he would just look at me. Sometimes, I'd catch a slight grin, but then it would quickly disappear. To my delight, though, he was always eager to read. Fiercely determined, he would make his way to the bookshelf and find a book, and then we would sit and painstakingly go through sounding out word after word. He did not give up. He did not get frustrated. He *tried*. One word at a time.

Friday, June 4, 2010

During this morning's sessions, Paul and I embarked on making a book like David's. It was a slower process, but Paul was engaged and excited. He drew a house with a mother, two sisters, and himself on the cover.

"What are your sisters' names?" I asked.

"Susan and Lois."

"S-U-S-A-N." Slowly, he scribed his sister's name, pausing at each letter to confirm. "Yes. Yes." He smiled, his teeth a brilliant white against his dark skin. His eyes sparkled. "L-O-I-S." And he nodded his head at each stroke of the purple marker. The book became a window into Paul's life, complete with a cow and chickens and a garden and all the responsibilities that went with them.

As we continued to work on English, Paul and I sat on a blanket in the backyard working with flash cards. I laid out three cards—*I* and *S* and *H*—and made the "ish" sound, prompting Paul to repeat it. Then we added a D in front to make the word DISH. I showed him a dish from the kitchen and he understood. We added F to make FISH and then drew a picture of a fish. He got it. Without thinking, I added a W at the front of the three letters and said "WISH," feeling a bit bewildered over how I would draw that. Paul looked back at me, clearly puzzled.

"What is that?" he asked.

Hum, that's tricky, I thought. I tried to explain to him, "A wish is when you ask for something special, something beyond what you would ordinarily have. Something big.

Something really important." I paused to let it sink in. "If a magic fairy offered you one wish, what would it be?"

Paul sat silently for some time. I had learned to give him his space, allowing him time to ponder questions. The deep green trees swayed in the wind and the scent of the freshly tilled dirt from the garden filled my nostrils. I stared at this little boy and grinned as he continued to ponder my question. Seconds turned into minutes, and time stood still as we sat on that blanket on a hill in rural Kenya.

"A toilet," he whispered.

These were the moments that captured me, these moments when reality was presented to me in the most humble way possible, in the form of a beautiful young boy just wanting a little more for himself and his family. We drew a toilet in his book and carried on with our project.

It wasn't until much later that a thought crossed my mind. Simply by my having this conversation with him, Paul may have assumed that I could produce a toilet for him. While trying to help, I may have unwittingly created unrealistic expectations. I was ignorant of my actions and the damage I could do.

Thoughts of my other life bubbled up randomly. Sweet Margaret, a thirteen-year-old stroke survivor, came into the volunteer room this afternoon. She cuddled up with me on the lounge chair and showed me her writing. It was a prayer to God. She thanked him for making trees because they provided shade for us to sit under, they made berries for animals to eat, and they gave us wood to make furniture. I couldn't help but smile. If only my furniture industry friends could see this. It was definitely a far cry from flipping chairs in waiting rooms.

My Blackberry was still my regular form of communication with people in the States. As long as my device was charged, I received emails daily. The time difference made for delayed responses, but it still worked.

I recently received a note from a friend, Melissa, who has a friend who was recently diagnosed with breast cancer. She had started chemotherapy the day before and Melissa was looking for advice on how to be a good support person. It was so easy to reminisce and make suggestions. I remembered all the wonderful, giving things people did for me, like grocery shopping, cleaning my house, taking me out to breakfast, cooking for me, and just plain listening to me bitch. They had rearranged furniture, and sent scarves, books, and pretty-smelling body lotions. They had sent subscriptions for *People* magazine and delivered pizza for lunch. So many thoughtful gestures, and each one of them equally important. It was easy to advise her on this subject.

As the group of volunteers and matrons became more like a cohesive family, I shared pictures with my new friends from when I'd been bald and talked a bit about my cancer journey. It was bridging a mental canyon. Being at Hilltop had been so intense that thoughts of doctors and meds and surgeries had slowly dissipated. There were no TVs promoting cancer centers. There were no pink ribbons or survivor events. It was an oasis from the massive media content focused on this disease.

Auntie Joyce looked at my new growth hair and suggested I get a weave—just like her.

"Oh boy," I laughed. "I don't know, Joyce. That looks like a lot of work."

"It's not bad, Auntie. You will look so smart. I will take you to the salon and you will have long hair again. Yes, yes. We will do this tomorrow."

After much persuasion, I agreed, probably more interested in being part of the community than in having extensions put in.

The following day, I spent six hours in a bad chair while three women pulled at the stubble growing out of my head. As each new client walked into the salon, a buzz of activity would start up in their native tongues.

Once in a while, I would catch the word "mzungu" and I would pipe up.

"I know you are talking about me. What are you saying?"

The gaggle of women would all laugh and joke, and someone would translate for me. A day at the salon was not easy for me. It was actually physical torture sitting in that seat. As my new friends tugged and twisted at my mzungu hair, all I could think about was how grateful I was to even have hair. And the cost for three women to work on my hair for six hours? Seven dollars. I didn't even negotiate it.

Friday, June 11, 2010

Activity was swirling at the house on the hill. The Day of the African Child was happening next weekend and momentum was building. Dozens of people were coming from the States: the founders of Hilltop Children's Home, more volunteers, and some adventure junkies who were set on climbing Kilimanjaro as a fundraiser for the organization. People were sleeping on floors, on sofas, and in tents. The kids were bouncing off the walls with excitement. Joyce and Phoebe and Rebecca had prepared rice and lentils and beans by the tub full. Bruce was in overload, with his cellphone strapped to his head most of the time organizing last minute details. Charlie, one of the founders, would be on national Kenyan news promoting the event. Five hundred T-shirts were being delivered to hand out to first attendees. Three thousand bananas were stacked in a storage room.

There was a lot going on.

Over the past month, I had developed a deep respect and admiration for twenty-five-year-old Bruce Johnson. Day by day, he taught me about life in Naivasha. His calm, humble, intelligent demeanor had given me permission to spread my wings in a community that I had been deathly afraid of upon arrival. I had become comfortable in my new community. This event would be a shining moment for this young man, and I would help him however I could.

"I need you to mobilize the town for this event," he said, smirking. "Invite everyone in town to our party. Especially the people in the neighborhood around the new school."

Hmm. Inviting people to a party. That should be pretty easy, I thought. Except that most of the people in the neighborhood didn't speak English—a small stumbling block.

I gathered up a small group of new volunteers—Devon, Brendan, Savannah, and Tricia—and asked if they would help. They were enthusiastic college kids who had just landed in Naivasha and were willing to assist in any way possible. Our troop went out in search of Joyce and Phoebe, who were sitting on the lawn behind the house sorting rice and beans. We plopped down next to them and told them of our task.

"We need to invite the neighbors near the school to our party. Do you know anyone there?" I asked.

The women looked at me and smiled. "You?"

"Yeah. We are all going over to the school to make sure people feel welcome to come. Bruce wants us to."

"You will need to speak Kikuyu," Joyce said.

"Okay. How? Will you teach us?"

"*Shukuru Jeru*," she replied. "That is Kikuyu for *New School*."

"What?"

"Shu-ku-ru Jer-U," she repeated, a bit slower.

On a small scrap of paper, she wrote the words. Phonetically, they didn't make sense—at least not to my American English ear. I scratched out my own spelling based on the sounds. Joyce wrote more:

"Jimmie Gait ni aroka." Which meant, "Jimmie Gait is coming."

"Hiroko oshi." Translation: "Come tomorrow."

With the piece of paper stuffed in my pocket and a bunch of homemade flyers dispersed amongst our group, we headed out to mobilize Naivasha. John, my regular motorbike driver, was programmed into my Kenyan phone.

He was a pleasant and friendly young man who spoke English I could understand.

"Wi mwega, John." I smiled into the phone when he picked up.

"Nikwega," he said, and I could hear him smiling back.

"We need a ride to the "other side"—five of us. Can you and your friends come?"

"Yes. Yes. We'll be right there."

Within minutes, three motorbikes were at the gate. Our group piled onto the bikes—sometimes three per vehicle including the driver. Down the hill, around the donkeys, through town. Smiles of delight clear on each face, our posse was dropped at the bottom of the hill, about a mile from the new school.

"Asante sana rafiki. We'll call you in a while for a ride home. Yes?"

John smiled. "Asante sana." *Thank you.*

There we stood. On a dirt road surrounded by cabbage patches and sporadic homes and trees shaped like pompom trees. We practiced our lines.

"Shikuru Jera. Hiroko oshi. Jimmie Gait ni aroka."

I hoped we were saying it all right. We nodded at each other, full of self-congratulation, and laughed as we butchered such simple words. We were trying.

Devon, Tricia, and Savannah headed off down one path, and Brendan and I headed the other way. Divide and conquer. We had a lot of work to do.

At the first farm, a woman off in the distance was hoeing the soil.

"Wi mwega," I greeted her and waved. "Kuja hapa." *Hello, and, come here please.*

She smiled, waved back, placed her tool gently against the fence, and made her way to the gate. I guess I said the right thing.

Brendan looked at the piece of paper and recited the six words.

She nodded and said, "Kikuyu?" Implying, "You speak Kikuyu?"

We made a sign with our fingers as if to say, "a little." Her face broke out in a smile. We shook hands and pointed in the direction of the new school.

"Ni aroka." *Tomorrow.* "Kuina." *Dance.*

I shook my hips and moved my arms around a bit, smiling a lot. The woman's head flew back as a belly laugh escaped her mouth.

"Kuina, Kuina." She nodded. "Mzungu kuina."

Dance. Dance. White people dance. I guess she thought that was funny.

This was just the beginning of our adventure into the Aberdare Mountains. Brendan and I entered many wooden gates, strolled into people's homes, visited their shambas—gardens—got offered tea numerous times, smiled, shook hands, and repeated the words, "Shukuru jera. Jimmie Gait ni aroka. Kuina. Kuina."

Neighbors waited for us as we made our way through the hills.

"Wi mwega," we said to anyone we saw. They responded with "Nik wega" and a smile, and then a long string of words. Brendon and I would nod and smile and repeat, "Shukuru jera. Jimmie Gait ni aroka."

People were happy. For hours, we walked the hills and shook hands and smiled and laughed and watched cows poop in the road. We promoted and promoted and promoted. Eventually, our paths crossed with Tricia, Devon, and Savannah, and the stories flew. *The man with a tumor the size of a grapefruit sticking out of his neck had asked the girls in for tea. The family with nine kids running around and dancing in the yard screaming, "Mzungu, mzungu, mzungu."*

The woman who looked to be ninety with no teeth tilling her garden and offering up a head of cabbage to her visitors. We had invited the community to our party, and they had invited us into their homes. Now, we just had to wait and see if they would come.

Sunday, June 13, 2010

At 5:30 on Saturday morning, the sky looked ominous.

"Please don't rain. Please don't rain," we all chanted.

Batches of eggs and loaves of toast were made for hoards of people who were strewn throughout the house. One by one, they arrived in the kitchen and the tasks for the day were dispensed: decorate the site, make sure the generator arrived on "the other side," mobilize people in town, pick up more chairs, get the tents set up, unload the three thousand bananas, set up the speakers, make sure the transport vehicle had arrived, gather everyone at the KCB Bank, and decorate the vehicle that would lead the procession.

The house was in production mode. The kids were getting dressed in their Hilltop Children's Home T-shirts. Radio ads were running. We had no idea what this would turn into. Fingers were double-crossed. I really hoped it would be a successful event. Bruce had worked so hard on it.

I had heard it said that Kenyans were not an early morning people, but it wasn't true on this day.

At 7:00 a.m., crowds started to gather in front of the KCB Bank. Children of all ages were dressed in their school uniforms and gathered in color-coordinated groups along the streets. All the shops were closed for the day, and slowly our little gathering started to grow. The radio station and the celebrity DJ who would be broadcasting the live event arrived. There were TV crews, motorbikes, face painters, and clowns. Balloons and banners were hitched on the bikes and the trucks. Kids wore red, black, and green T-shirts, representing the colors of the Kenyan flag. I watched as people entered the main street from all directions. There must have been five hundred people gathered at the junction already.

"What do you need me to do?" I asked Bruce.

"Go to the other side and see if you can organize whoever is over there."

Tricia and I hopped a motorbike and headed to the Caltex Petrol station on the other side of town. As we made our way down the valley, across the bridge and up the hill, my heart beat through my chest. There were people everywhere. The whole town was out, and the masses were gathering. Blue, red, and green school uniforms moved as clusters along the streets. People had signs reading "Day of the African Child" and "HOPE." Grey clouds hung in the distance.

Tricia and I got off the bikes and found Peter Murimi, one of the businessmen on the planning committee. He was talking to the chief, who was a giant of a man.

"Ah. Peter. What a great day!" I smiled as I greeted him with a kiss on each cheek. "Congratulations, Chief. You must be so proud." I shook his hand as he nodded in response.

"Naivasha is a good place. We are happy Hilltop Children's Home is here," exclaimed the mountain of a man standing in front of me.

"It wasn't just Hilltop Children's Home. It was the entire committee. Look at this! It's amazing!!" I smiled, knowing the entire community had been involved in planning the event.

A feeling of elation filled the air. Tricia and I stood at the Caltex station watching buses of students arrive as the police directed the mass of traffic. The group that had congregated at the Gimwa was making its way across the bridge and up the hill. Music was blaring. Kids were singing. Bruce's blonde hair and white skin jumped out of a sea of people. Our eyes connected for a split second and we exchanged thumbs-ups. It was another one of those moments. This young man was teaching me about unconditional love, and I felt like I was in the presence of something magical. Tears dribbled down my face.

The town was celebrating the Day of the African Child. It was acknowledging the importance of education, and with that a hope for a better future. It was estimated that roughly two thousand people made their way along the two-mile stretch through the village, over the hills, and to the rural area that housed our new school. The paved road ended and the procession made its way up the dirt hill. People of all ages held hands, sang songs, and shouted, "Jimmy Gait!"

The crowd rounded a corner then and, directly in front of us, stood the bright white, two-story, all-window structure that held the future of some of these children in its hands. It looked like a diamond shining in the sun.

The schoolyard was framed by tall pine trees, lush green pastures, and a thin brook. A few small houses with rusted metal roofs were scattered throughout the area. Thousands of people funneled into the front lawn and found seats on the fresh, green grass. Chairs were available for the elderly, and tents kept others out of the sun. Excited children gathered with their friends and chatted incessantly.

As the masses settled in, Bruce appeared on the roof of the school, microphone in hand, to welcome the community to the Day of The African Child. Applause rang out and the hillside shook. Politicians were introduced one by one and their long, drawn-out speeches promoted the value of the next generation, as well as their individual platforms. The community was used to listening to the endless speeches of politicians. Meanwhile, the sky was getting darker and the air a little cooler.

Winners of the school poetry contests were called to the stage to deliver their messages. A tiny eleven-year-old stood strong atop the white two-story structure and spoke confidently of faith, knowledge, growth, and overcoming obstacles. He was eloquent beyond his years, and fearless in his presentation and resolution. He belted out his message of hope for an education that would carry him and his family through life. He used words like *perseverance*, *persistence*, and *progress*. Eleven years old! Dressed in a green sweater and grey shorts and neatly polished black shoes. Nothing could stop this kid. All he needed was to catch a break. Two thousand people applauded his efforts, and as he walked off the stage, he seemed to stand a little taller.

I had plopped myself down in the middle of the crowd, soaking up the energy. In a country that was far away from my home, in a place where I didn't know a soul, in a culture where I didn't belong, I was content.

The long-awaited main event, Jimmie Gait, was finally upon us. Young girls were busting at the seams. There was a celebrity in town, and the town was going to have a party. Just like at every big opening in the States, fireworks were shot off to create that festive, thrilling adrenaline rush. Bruce hadn't quite anticipated the crowd's reaction, though. As the *bang, bang, bang* of the fireworks blasted in the air, the crowd screamed fearfully and dropped to the ground. People made mad dashes for cover. Some scoured the field to see if there was anything else happening. Fireworks sounded really similar to gunshots.

This was definitely a cultural faux pas. An announcement was immediately made to explain that the noises had been fireworks, which were a means of celebration. Thousands of people exhaled and relaxed back into the party. Jimmie Gait made his way to the stage. Music rang from the speakers across the fields and the entire lawn got to its feet, screaming and clapping. Unfortunately, at that exact moment, the skies opened up and rain started to drench the crowd.

But it didn't matter.

Jimmie sang "Huratiti," a well-known pop song complete with its own dance moves. Masses moved in unison as the lawn became a mosh pit. Two thousand people sang the chorus in unison. Hilltop Children's Home scholars danced on the rooftop. Elderly women held plastic chairs over their heads as makeshift umbrellas. No one was phased by the weather. It was the rainy season and to be expected. The show went on as planned, full of laughter, smiles, and dancing in the rain.

The point had been made. Hilltop Children's Home cared about educating children and was part of the community.

It took a full week to recover after the celebration. The house emptied out a bit, people left for other parts of the world, and the town quieted down once more. Our family settled back into its normal routine: breakfast, school, homework, washing socks, dinner, reading time, movies, and bedtime. Helen, David, and Paul kept my days full, as did trips to town in search of five-cent bananas or seventy-cent pineapples.

Over time, I had developed friendships with some of the local shopkeepers and would often pop in for tea and a Kikuyu lesson while reading the local paper. The regulars would teach me about the politics of the country, the forty-two tribes, and the riots of 2007. Discussions centered around HIV education, agriculture in the area, the weather, and the Chinese influence in the construction industry.

The locals wanted to teach me Kikuyu. Knowing Swahili was one thing, but knowing Kikuyu… well, that was something entirely different. Over a cup of tea, Mary, the owner of a cafe, would sound out words and patiently correct me as I tried to make the right noises come out of my mouth. She would smile pleasantly, nod her head, and we would sip chai.

My Kikuyu vocabulary grew slowly. John the motorbike driver would quiz me by pointing to a dog. I would respond with "ngoe." He taught me the words for donkey and chicken and motorbike. Languages had never been my strong suit, but I wanted to try. People were kind and patient, though, helping me.

Sunday, June 25, 2010

The kids from Hilltop Children's Home were often treated to field trips if their school marks were good and if everyone had been on their best behavior. One such trip was a visit to Hell's Gate, a not-so-distant national park complete with a drive-through safari—something similar to our version of a Busch Gardens, except with no gates and no shopkeepers.

We piled the whole family, complete with neighborhood kids and packed picnic lunches, into a rented bus. The matrons were dressed in their Sunday best and the kids were anxiously awaiting their first glimpse of a zebra or a warthog. It was an hour-and-a-half of another African massage on a bumpy road, but no one complained.

The entrance to the park was a stone archway with a hand-carved sign reading "Hell's Gate." Sam the bus driver parked our rig in the designated lot, and sixteen kids, ten college students, three matrons, and a bus driver piled out of the blue bus. It was not your typical family unit or the ordinary day at the beach. Our entourage gathered around the ticket sale counter, each child looking for their pass. As the entrance stubs were dispersed, *Thank yous* were heard from sixteen little people. Oftentimes, this phrase was followed by "I love you."

Our herd headed to the picnic area. Peanut butter and jelly sandwiches were distributed along with cut-up bananas. Again, *Thank yous* were plentiful. Following lunch, the buddy system was enacted and the hike through the park made progress. The word "hike" takes on a different meaning when it's used in the same sentence as the phrase "sixteen kids." This was more like a walk along a dusty road, though. Most of the kids were excited about the adventure, but in a group this large, nothing is perfect.

"I just can't go on," panted Margaret. "It's too hard."

Margaret always struggled. She was ten years old and had suffered a stroke three months after being born. Life had not gotten any easier for this child: her parents died, her uncle was abusive, her physical health failed, the left side of her body had residual damage from the stroke, and her emotional issues would flare up at any given moment. Hilltop Children's Home had been a saving grace for her, as it was for all these children. It was easy to sometimes forget about their difficulties. I held Margaret's hand, kissed her cheek, and told her how strong she was. We moved on step by step, Margaret's limp leg dragging in the dirt along the way.

At the ten-minute mark, an executive decision was made to head back to the bus. Children, women, and young adults clambered back into the vehicle. Instead of "hiking," we would do a driving safari. Zebras dotted the fields. Warthogs looked like black pigs with horns. Giraffes stared off into the distance. Antelope and gazelle roamed around the open area.

"Auntie, Auntie. A zebra!" Margaret pointed to the black and white animals grazing in the field. Her smile was glorious, as was the feeling of excitement from inside the bus. Matthew and Leonard hung their heads out the window, pointing at the wildlife. Brendan, Devon, and Tricia were covered in kids and full of smiles. Auntie Joyce, Auntie Rebecca, and Mom sat calmly in the front of the bus taking in the sights.

As with anything, the novelty of black and white striped animals wears off pretty quickly. Towards the end of the loop, a sign pointed the way to a lower gorge. It was a great opportunity to get out of the bus and do something that was actually close to a hike. Most of the kids wanted to check it out (*most* being the key word), but this trek involved a few obstacles and some technical climbing. Only the big kids could go: Josh, Matthew, Charlotte, Ava, Jim, and David, to be accompanied by the volunteers, of course. The younger and smaller children stayed with the matrons and had a short rest in the shade. I opted for the mini-hike.

The narrow footpath followed a bubbling brook through overgrown forests. Miniature monkeys sat high atop the trees and the sun was eclipsed by the density of the foliage. Eventually, the green of the jungle transitioned into a dark, narrow valley of rock shooting straight up on either side of the creek.

"Be careful. Hold onto the walls," I called out as the agile kids bounced along the trail and I sat my butt on a ledge to gently lower myself to the next level.

"Auntie, are you okay?" Charlotte asked as I fell to the end of the line.

"Yeah. I'm good, sweets. Just be careful, please."

Being a parent must be so hard.

Tricia and I laughed as we moved along the winding path, noticing the drop in temperature. Eventually, the valley opened to a small pool of water. From the rock wall, a spring of water dribbled out in a mini waterfall. It reminded me of home, of the geysers in Saratoga, and of how similar places are even when they are worlds apart.

As we approached the small stream, Josh put his hand under the water.

"Ouch," he cried out, quickly drawing back his hand. "It's hot." Matthew and Ava and David all ran to the spring to touch the water. Each of them pulled their hands from the hot stream, giggling.

"It's hot. It's hot. There's hot water here," they shrieked.

I stuck my fingers under the water. Sure enough, it was a hot spring—piping hot, almost boiling hot. I suddenly remembered the fault lines and the volcanic activity that ran beneath the rift valley, and explained this to Josh.

I was learning more than anticipated during these field trips. My world was expanding exponentially by the day.

Thoughts of sinuous spring seat construction, video conferencing tables, and delivery dates were a thing of the distant past.

Wednesday, June 30, 2010

Earlier this week, I made a trip to Nairobi to run errands for the house. When I returned, little Rainboot Regina stood in the yard with a smile spread from ear to ear. She ran to me and wrapped her arms around me. I was genuinely confused, but thrilled to see her. Regina had made her way into the hearts of the decision-makers at Hilltop Children's Home. She had been roaming around town for too long and she needed some stability. She would be coming to school at our facility.

On her first day of class, Regina and I walked into class one, the class full of little kids. She would be learning basic English and Swahili with children much younger than her, and yet she would be afforded the opportunity to be educated. She was measured for a new uniform and was given new socks and shoes. I wasn't sure what emergency plan had been put in place to deal with her epilepsy, but I was confident that the individuals here could handle the situation.

Three medical students from Dallas had recently arrived at our house on the hill. Preparations had been made for these doctors in training to administer physical exams for all the family children, as well as the day scholars. Medical records were being established. Each child was weighed and measured. Their eyes, ears, noses, and throats were checked. Their bodies were examined and blood sticks were done for HIV screening. Constant rainy weather, torn shoes, wet socks, and unclean water ate away at the soles of the children's feet.

Tricia, a nursing student, marked the charts as one child after another was marched into the makeshift exam room. Her sad eyes looked at me as I wandered through the space.

"I can't believe their feet," she said as she stripped off the mud-caked socks and exposed gaping holes oozing puss and dirt. Peterson, a mischievous, adorable eight-year-old, smiled warmly at me as Tricia cleaned his feet and applied antibacterial ointment and wrapped his heals in gauze.

"Hey, Peterson," I said with a smile. "What's going on?"

This kid was one of the most rambunctious of the crowd, and his sheer boyishness constantly touched my heart. He also reminded me of the beauty of NOT being a mother. I rubbed the top of his head and headed to the store room in search of socks and shoes that could be dispersed to our day scholars.

Later that evening, after all the school kids had returned home and the Hilltop Children's Home kids were having dinner, the volunteers unwound in the far kitchen. Laptops were out. Blackberries were buzzing. Photos were being downloaded and blogs were being updated. Conversations revolved around the health and wellness of children. Susan was one of the newest children to join our family and had just arrived the week prior. She was nine years old, and the day's testing had revealed that she was HIV positive.

"Thank God she came to us when she did," Bruce commented. "She's so lucky."

I hadn't considered this perspective. My initial reaction had been one of sadness rather than gratitude. But his point made sense. Untreated children usually died from HIV at a very early age. Instead, Susan would get the treatment she needed and her health would be properly monitored because she was part of our family. The alternative was difficult to imagine, but a normal part of the landscape within this society.

Friday, July 2, 2010

Each day brought its own trials and tribulations: rain, mud, food, school, fifteen kids, or even lack of water because an elephant crushed the water pipe in the forest. Normal stuff. But each evening after the kids were in bed, the volunteers sat together and commiserated and laughed, and agreed that this life was worth living. On one particular evening, Mom knocked on the door as she entered the volunteer room.

"Uncle Bruce?" The hard lines of her face were a paradox to the softness of her demeanor.

"Yes, Mom?" His admiration for this woman was obvious.

"I need to tell you about Jim." Her British accent was musical as she stood in the doorway.

"Come. Sit with us." He patted the seat beside him.

Mom entered the room and perched herself on the arm of the blue upholstered sofa as the volunteers all stared into the screens of their laptops and Blackberries, connecting with the other side of the world.

"I walked into the kitchen today and found Jim standing by himself. He was staring off into space, silent and still. It was so unlike him. I thought he was ill. I was concerned and asked if there was something wrong. He continued to stare out the window as if in a trance and calmly responded, 'I was just thinking about how much I suffered before and how much I have now.'"

Everyone stopped what they were doing and looked up. I glanced in the direction of Bruce and Phoebe.

Jim had come to Hilltop Children's Home in January of that year, just six months earlier. For two years prior, he had been sleeping behind the shops at night and eating out of the trash. He was a beautiful, intelligent, energetic boy full of life and curiosity. He was constantly smiling and laughing. Gratitude poured from his tiny body, and when he walked into a room, the space lit up. To hold his hand was to know true love.

"Oh, Mom," Bruce said, smiling. "Is he okay now?"

"Yes. He is good. I just wanted to let you know." She squeezed Bruce's shoulder and left the room.

For a brief second, silence hung in the air. We glanced at each other and smiled. It was life as usual at Hilltop Children's Home. Amazing things happened here every day.

Saturday, July 3, 2010

The Village Market Mall was an upscale area of Nairobi where the diplomats and expats gathered. It was also the destination for a Saturday family "good-behavior" excursion. Fifteen kids and just as many adults spilled from the big blue, painted tour bus into the mall parking lot after a two-hour ride from Naivasha. Each child had been given two hundred shillings for spending money. That was the equivalent of two dollars each. The buddy system was implemented and each volunteer was assigned a pair of kids to look after before we entered Nakumatt, a Kenyan version of Walmart. David and Rose became my partners. Our threesome wandered the aisles full of clothes, toys, candy, and food.

"Auntie, can I buy this?" David asked as he pulled a chocolate bar from the shelf. "Or this?" he asked as his other hand held up a pack of gum.

"Is that what you really want?"

He wasn't sure. He couldn't commit. He put the pack of gum back on the shelf and we made our way to the next aisle. Rose's English wasn't very good, and David would speak to her in Kikuyu as their eyes surveyed the shelves and they touched one item after another—pencils, marbles, stickers, socks. Rose smiled and clung to my hand. The money was clearly burning holes in their pockets.

In the end, David settled on a plastic horse and Rose picked a set of markers. We made our way through the checkout line as each child paid for their purchase separately. They carried their white plastic shopping bags proudly into the main corridor of the mall as we met up with the rest of the group.

A small pet store was located across the corridor from Nakumatt. Inside were six oversized aquariums filled with blue, yellow, orange, and green fish of all shapes and sizes. The children completely infiltrated the small space. Fingers pointed in every direction and the kids gazed in amazement at the swimming creatures in front of them. They moved from tank to tank and back again to make sure everyone saw the blowfish, the eels, the catfish, and the wavy coral. Forty-five minutes later, the newness of colored fish wore off and the mass of children made their way out of the fish store and headed down the hall.

A toy store three doors down became the next stop on the tour of the mall. The girls made a beeline to the pink section, trying on boas and tiaras and posing for pictures as if on the red carpet. The boys were immediately drawn to the wall of cars and trucks, and a remote-control Corvette became the catalyst for something close to an emotional catastrophe. Leonard held the plastic box close to his chest as he asked, "Auntie, will you buy this for me?"

"No. Sorry, Leonard. You can't have the remote-control car."

"But Auntie... I want it SO BADLY."

"Yes, yes, I know, Leonard. But not today. Please put it back." My lack of mothering experience was obvious at this juncture. Crocodile tears welled up in his cute, loveable eyes.

Then David joined in. Then Matthew.

"Please, Auntie. We would really like this car. We love it so much."

"Not today, boys. I think we are done with this store. Let's go." I took Leonard's hand and walked away from the back wall, hoping to escape the toy store before a meltdown of gigantic proportions erupted. As Leonard sniffled his way through the hallway and gave me the cold shoulder, the scene reminded me, *This is what it's like to be a parent.*

At the far end of the mall was a gate. Once our entire family had regrouped, we paid the admission price at the ticket counter and made our way into another adventure.

"Where are we?" Heather asked.

"At the water park," Bruce said.

"The what?" she pushed.

"Look up," he said, pointing. "See all those big tubes? They are filled with water and you get to ride down them."

"In the dark?"

"Yep. Don't worry. You'll be fine. It's fun."

The kids timidly walked past the slides and the small pools, heading towards the restrooms. Joyce, Phoebe, and Rebecca had packed bathing suits for everyone.

In the locker room, Lynn and Helen discovered the automatic dryer on the wall and pushed the round silver button. The loud noise startled them. I stuck my hand underneath it to show them it was all right. They looked at each other, giggled, and then stuck their hands and their heads under the nozzle. Within minutes, there was a crowd surrounding the device and Margaret, Rose, Susan, and Ava were dancing under the dryer in their bathing suits.

"Okay, okay, girls. That's enough. Let's go swim," I urged them, ushering them out from underneath the dryer. I was such a stick in the mud.

The buddy system was enacted once again and each kid got a volunteer. Timidly, the kids climbed one by one to the top of the slides, skeptically looking at the tubes. Joyce, Phoebe, Rebecca, and I sat on the picnic bench, watching as the kids cautiously approached the tubes, just like real mothers would. Pair by pair, one of the college-aged volunteers and a child would sit themselves on the cold blue plastic slide.

The tunnels were enclosed, but the sound of the kids coming down was like a pack of animals screaming in the fields. As each pair made its way into the light, expressions of pure excitement flooded their faces. Water splashed everywhere, followed by shrieks of adrenaline and non-stop laughter. Up and down they went. Kid after kid. Screaming and splashing with excitement.

Billy was the first to stop. He was cold and shaking. HIV caused his body temperature to drop quickly. His lips shivered and he cuddled up next to Phoebe with a warm blanket and a dry pair of clothes. He sat with us on the benches and watched his brothers and sisters continue their adventure. The older kids lasted longer than the little ones, but gradually they each got worn out and made their way to us for their warm clothes.

They kept repeating, "Thank you! Thank you, Uncle Bruce." It was a friend of Bruce's family who had subsidized the trip.

At the food court, tables were rearranged to accommodate the herd and pizzas were ordered. Big screens in the middle of the open environment played last night's World Cup football game. The boys were instantly entranced, and pretty soon the girls were, too.

Back home, this would have been an ordinary day at the mall, and yet I was seven thousand miles away from ordinary. I was in the middle of Kenya. I scanned the faces of the children and watched them interact with each other, merrily chomping away on their slices of pizza. These kids didn't have parents. One of them had been left to die in the forest. Others had almost been boiled alive by their mother. There was abuse, neglect, malnutrition, hunger, and disease floating through the background of this group of children. But you couldn't see it as they ate their pizza while watching the World Cup game. And there was no way that I would have seen it from seven thousand miles away. It was a showing of resilience, of strength, and of enduring love.

It was magic.

At the end of the day, we loaded back onto the bus with all the commotion and racquet that happens whenever a herd like ours moved around. The kids settled into their seats and prepared for the ride home. I really hoped they would take naps. I was exhausted. But, no such luck. The kids immediately started chatting about the wonderful day they had just had.

Before we left the lot, Phoebe asked, "What was your favorite part of today?"

I listened intently, assuming it would be the water slides, the pizza, or the ice cream they got at the end of dinner.

Jim answered first. "The pet store!"

"Yeah, me too! The fish. The fish." They all agreed.

God, I loved these kids. They kept things simple, and really shifted my perspective.

Sunday, July 4, 2010

Sunday was the Fourth of July. Tricia and Devon and I made our inaugural trip to the Full Gospel Church with Joyce and the kids. We packed the pews at the back of the church, kids on top of kids on top of volunteers. People turned and stared. Children from the village made sideways glances at the mzungus in their church and then quickly looked away when our eyes would meet.

Dorkus, the proprietor of Wisdom Café, a local internet café, was asked to be the translator for the service. Groups of children from different schools made their way to the front of the church and performed for the congregation. Tricia, Devon, and I looked at each other with surprise when the Hilltop Children's Home kids were called to the stage. We had no idea they had been preparing for a performance.

They sang and danced and smiled and carried on like troopers in front of the mass of people. None of them were intimidated or shy. *When did they practice this stuff? How come we didn't know about it?* I supposed the matrons and teachers had helped them during the day. So much happened at the house that we weren't aware of.

From the back of the church, the three of us cheered on our kids like proud mothers. Naivasha had never heard such loud applause. We hugged each child as they returned to their seats. It was probably a spectacle, but we didn't care. We were so proud of them.

After their performance, everyone settled back into their seats. Lynn Obama cuddled up on my lap and Regina sat to my right. Auntie Joyce was seated in front of us with Susan. Regina quietly leaned over the pew and murmured something to Joyce. A short, whispered conversation ensued. Regina then stood up, got out of the pew, and left the church. I shot a concerned glance at Joyce, and then to the door where Regina had just exited.

I wanted to ask Joyce where Regina was going, but couldn't disrupt church or make an even bigger commotion than we already had. Whatever it was that was happening, Joyce had handled it, but I was still worried.

The service continued in Kikuyu and hard-to-understand English for two hours. My rump started to hurt from the wooden benches. I shifted awkwardly, trying to balance Lynn on my lap while also trying to find a more comfortable position.

I heard the words, "Trust God. He will provide. He cares for all people."

"Amen."

As we left the building, I rushed to Joyce.

"Where did Regina go?"

"Her parents were in church. They wanted her to get her things."

Was that safe? I wondered. Regina, an eleven-year-old, was going to her father's house, and this was a man who had beaten her and sold her when she'd been nine years old. Obviously, though, Joyce knew what she was doing. Our group gathered together to make its way home. It was lunchtime, and there were chores to do.

Ten minutes later, we found Regina standing at the edge of the road waiting for us. She was holding a small plastic shopping bag full of everything she owned. Her face was expressionless as she fell into line next to me. I reached down and put my hand on her shoulder affectionately as we trudged upward through the mud. My understanding of the culture was minimal, and it was difficult to internalize what was happening. I was witnessing life from a perspective different than my own, and I had to work on accepting differences as they were.

Love and tolerance of others became my core belief.

Later that afternoon, twelve visitors arrived at the center—eight Scottish and four Kenyan scouts. Dressed in blue and white neckties, these young adults pitched their bright green tents in the backyard along the cabbage patch.

Since it was the Fourth of July, a small party had been planned to celebrate American independence. A sheep was slaughtered, skinned, and roasted. Kids gathered around and participated as much as was allowed. Dining tables were moved to the backyard and set up picnic-style. Buckets of rice, lentils, salad, and fruit were placed in a buffet line. Dinner was served.

Children, guests, matrons, and volunteers all found a place at the table. Before we ate, Josh stood and led us all in prayer.

"Lord, we thank you for this supper. God, remember those who don't have any. In Jesus' name we pray. Amen."

Then, people of all ages, colors, and cultures sat together and shared in the American tradition—a picnic in the backyard next to a cabbage patch. This was not the ordinary hamburgers, hot dogs, and strawberry shortcake version of a celebration, but it was a celebration nonetheless.

By nightfall, wood was stacked like a teepee for a bonfire while the kids went around gathering long sticks to roast marshmallows. Brendon and Devon diligently passed out safety instructions regarding the fire and roasting anything over it.

"What *is* that?" Auntie Joyce asked when she saw the marshmallow.

Auntie Phoebe shook her head vehemently when asked if she wanted to try one of the burnt puffy white balls.

"No, thank you," she said firmly. Marshmallows probably seem like pretty weird food options if you've never seen them before. It rather reminded me of my own aversion to mayonnaise.

The kids were mesmerized. Tricia and I couldn't unwrap packages of crackers and chocolate fast enough. Children raced to us, holding scorched marshmallows and anxiously pleading for us to make them a chocolate and cracker sandwich. What kids don't like sugar, right?

Shortly thereafter, guitars appeared as we all gathered around the fire. College-aged kids strummed away with the Beatles, Bruce Springsteen, and Led Zeppelin. It was anything but typical campfire music. The children were wrapped in blankets, and I sat on the ground with Regina seated next to me, her head leaning on my arm. The orange glow illuminated our eclectic family in the mountains of Kenya. The warmth radiated not only from the fire, but from the hearts of each person there.

Monday, July 5, 2010

The next morning, Tricia, Devon, and Brendan wheeled their luggage to the front lawn as they prepared for their departure. Kenneth, the driver, had arrived and was waiting with his white Corolla. Children assembled as if they were having a class picture taken, tall in the back and short in the front. They swayed back and forth as they sang about love and gratitude, wishing each person a safe journey home. It was the departure song.

A line was formed, and one by one the children approached Tricia, Devon, and Brendan. I stood back and watched, my heart breaking as hugs and kisses were exchanged. My feelings of impending separation anxiety streamed out of my eyes in the form of tears.

I said a quick goodbye to each of these college kids, gave them a hug, and then marched into the house looking for someplace to hide, someplace that would shelter me from these emotions… someplace where no one would see me cry. I didn't want my new friends to leave, but even more than that, I didn't want to leave.

My departure was scheduled for the following week. I was acutely aware that I had found a new home and a new family. I had come to love the hills of Naivasha. Lack of warm water wasn't as bad as it sounded. Not when, every once in a while, a ten-year-old grabbed my hand and looked in my eyes and said, "God bless you, Auntie Bethany. God bless you."

Tuesday, July 6, 2010

My brain started to enter return mode.

During my last trip to Nairobi, I purchased a cart full of matchbox cars, fancy handkerchiefs, and *High School Musical* sticker books. I bought bags full of socks and underwear.

When I returned to the house, I enthusiastically passed out the goodies. Each child kissed and hugged me with gratitude.

I shouldn't spoil them, I thought. But then I remembered some of the awful things these children had had to go through. They deserved a little spoiling.

As I sat in my room later that night, I wondered what it would be like to go back to America. No more donkeys or cows in the roads—paved roads. Electricity, twenty-four seven. People speaking English all day. Warm water. Temperatures over fifty degrees and pretty sundresses. Clean sundresses. Nice sheets. Empty house.

Thursday, July 8, 2010

Over the next two days, I tried to give away as much of what I had left as possible. Dresses went to Rebecca, Joyce, and Mom. Jewelry, hats, bandanas, lotions, lipsticks, nail polish... whatever I had, I gave away. I spent extra time with the kids whenever I could.

Charlotte grabbed my Blackberry and took dozens of pictures of herself. I ate every meal with the kids. I read book after book with any child who wanted to sit with me.

I didn't want to give them up.

When the day finally came for my departure, I made some really lame attempts at good-bye with the schoolkids and teachers. I kept it as brief and simple as possible for fear of bursting into tears at any moment.

As I said my individual farewells to the children, each one of them would ask the same question, "When will you be back?" They didn't ask "Are you coming back?" They asked, "When?" It was a much different question.

I'd never intended to come back a second time. That hadn't been part of my plan, and yet, as I looked into each one of their faces, the thought entered my mind, *"Wouldn't it be great to be with the kids at Christmas time."*

Sunday, July 11, 2010

Sunday morning, at four-thirty a.m., I pulled myself out of the bottom bunk for the last time, stripped the sheets, brushed my teeth, threw on whatever clothes were around, grabbed my luggage, and made my way to the tree stump at the front gate. The morning sky turned different shades of black, then blue, and then got a hint of orange. Chilly, rustic mountain air filled my lungs as the sound of Kenneth's car made my heart beat faster. Within seconds, he was inside the wooden gate. My bags were hurled into the trunk as I took one last glimpse at the stone house with Elephant Mountain in the background and the cabbage patch in the yard.

Deep down, I knew I would be back. I could't say good-bye permanently. "See you later" was a better answer.

I made my escape from Hilltop Children's Home before anyone was awake. It was just so much more peaceful that way. Avoidance was my coping mechanism.

Saturday, July 17, 2010

Sitting in the back corner of a coffee shop in Saratoga Springs, I disappeared into my laptop. In the midst of the crowds, the noise, the hustle and bustle, my screen transported me back to the other side of the world. Darling children smiled back at me. Music from the volunteer room played in my iPod. I stared at my five-dollar coffee and bagel, and shook my head. The money spent on this meal could have fed a family of six for three days in other parts of the world.

Attempting to return to "normal" was still on my To-Do list. A job. A paycheck. Business meetings. Dinner parties. A guy. Something stable. It didn't take long for me to be reminded that "normal" was an illusion, however, like quicksand. I had avoided going to the grocery store. I had avoided going to regular stores. I had avoided going where there were large groups and lots of lights. My insides didn't match my outsides.

Friends would ask me, "How was Africa?"

"Kenya was great," I would answer with a hint of exasperation. In my mind, the question was similar to asking someone who went to Florida, "How was North America?"

My responses became animated with stories of Margaret or Regina or David and a land far, far away. Most often, I believed people asked just to be polite. When I began to ramble on about the kids and my work there, their eyes would glaze over. I learned to offer short answers and then quickly shift conversations to the latest movie or the newest app for the iPhone. Even though I was physically back, I was disconnected and mentally detached from life in the States.

Now, I pushed my half-eaten bagel and coffee aside. A guy in a "Peace" T-shirt walked by and my automatic thought was, *What has HE done? How is HE trying to make the world a better place? He probably hasn't done ANYTHING, and yet he is walking around promoting something that he isn't willing to do anything about.*

I stopped myself short. Who did I think I was? I didn't have a clue about his story and the reason behind his T-shirt. Maybe he had spent years in Rwanda in the Peace Corps. Maybe he sent money every month to those in need. Maybe he sat with his ailing mother and held her hand every week. I didn't know anyone's story other than mine, and I had no right to judge others.

Sitting in the back corner of the coffee shop, I was humbled yet again.

That evening, I climbed into bed with Punky, Mazey, and my laptop. My cats snuggled in with me under the covers as I spent hours looking at Facebook pictures from the last ten weeks: a high school reunion I'd missed, a sorority reunion I'd been unable to attend... but, most importantly, hundreds of close-ups of smiling, happy kids from Hilltop Children's Home. My heart felt full.

I shut my laptop and nestled down under the sheets, my mind trying to put my past experiences into some kind of comprehensive format. Punky had crawled onto the pillow next to me and was purring in my ear.

Why did I really go to Kenya? What was I thinking? Why was I annoyed to be home? I wanted people to be as excited about this cause as I was. I wanted people to help. I wanted people to be interested and to start a movement.

I wanted world peace. Unfortunately, not everyone was on the same page.

My mind flashed back to days spent in bed when I couldn't move. Chemo had forced me to ask myself some tough questions, such as, "What is the purpose of my life?" In those moments of complete surrender, the answer had come. I just had to remember it and keep it in the front part of my brain.

I was supposed to be of service to others.

The message had taken on the form of children, filling my maternal instincts. I had been moved to "pay it forward" and to give away the love that had been so freely given to me during my cancer journey. As is typical during mid-life transformations, I had been pushed beyond my comfort zone. Kenya had saved me from myself. Living at Hilltop Children's Home had given my life perspective. Cancer began to look like a luxury disease, diagnosed only in wealthy countries. Sex had disappeared from my radar screen—well, almost. And, furniture? What about it? I had a new-found sense of gratitude and a deeper connection with the Big Guy upstairs.

I just needed to try to assimilate back into the world in which I'd been born.

Friday, August 13, 2010

Within a week of being back in the States, it was time to vacate my house again. The horses were back in Saratoga. It was time for me to become a nomad again. This year was different. There was no radiation. There were no daily visits to the hospital. This year, I was free.

My minivan became my home on wheels. I packed it with all the necessary clothes and accessories needed for a six-week stint on the road and parked it at a friend's house. My cats had been relocated to my parents' house again, and I was untethered.

I hopped on my Harley. Destination? Anywhere free. My savings account was dwindling, but my free spirit was unwilling to be shoved back into a box. I wandered the northeast, staying with friends, family, at campgrounds, and basking in my life and pretending I was riding a motorbike on the dirt roads of Naivasha.

Eventually, the seat of a two-wheeler lost its charm and I transferred my body to the old, reliable, beat-up, green minivan and headed to the comfort of my parents' house. I plopped onto the sofa in front of the TV and brushed the soft black and white fur of Punky and Mazey. I let Mom and Dad feed me, nurture me, and love me. My sister and her kids also popped in to visit a few times.

We watched movies, ate pizza, played cards, laughed, joked, and did nothing. It was another version of heaven on earth, and I settled in to the warmth of being with my family.

And during these happy moments, random happenings would remind me of Kenya.

In Naivasha, there was no excess. Everyone was respectful and appreciative of their belongings, whether that was a thatched roof hut, a cinderblock house, or a shed in the middle of the forest. Every morning at the center, the floors were swept and washed. Children washed their own socks when they returned home from school. The gardens were always tended to. The walkways were always clean. The rubbish was picked up off the ground. Everyone did the best they could with what they had.

My house on wheels—a.k.a. my minivan—needed a good cleaning. There was a definite stench brewing. Kenneth, our trusted Naivasha driver, would never have let his car get this disorderly. He would have been appalled.

It was time to get my shit together.

I cleaned everything—the windows, the dash, the doors, and even the dreaded cup holders. Carpet pads were tossed into the driveway and thoroughly detoxified. Upholstery cleaner was scrubbed into the floor carpet and mud was extracted. I was a pig. I was embarrassed. I was grateful I had a car.

Later, I sat staring at a laundry basket full of shoes. They were filthy and old. Surprisingly, "Time to go shopping" was not the first thought that entered my mind. Instead, images of Joyce and Phoebe and a handful of kids with black shoes and soap and scrub brushes filled my mind. I dumped the basket, lined up each pair of shoes on the driveway, and began cleaning them. The scrubbing bubbles settled into the funk from my feet and the sun beamed down on my shoulders. I didn't need to buy anything new. I had enough.

Dad came outside and sat in a lawn chair next to me.

"Whatcha' doing?" he asked curiously.

"It was time to clean some of my shit."

He smiled. Dad had always been frugal. I think he was pleased to watch me transition back to a simpler way of life.

After I was done, we sat together in the green-webbed folding chairs on the lawn, the smell of cleaning agents hanging in the air. Cars passed by. The blazing blue sky was a stark contrast to the brilliant green trees.

In a soft and calm voice, my dad said, "You know, I'm a pretty slow learner. It takes a long time for some things to sink into my head."

I scrunched my nose and turned to look at him. I was confused and somewhat stunned. This wasn't like any of the typical conversations I had with my dad.

"What are you talking about?"

His face was subdued as he looked out over the valley.

"When you first told me you were going to Kenya, I wasn't very supportive of it."

Uh oh. My dad and I were having a heart to heart. I hadn't planned on that. I was just trying to clean my shoes.

"Oh, Daddy, it's okay. It's not a big deal." I shrugged.

"I didn't understand." His voice cracked a bit, and all of a sudden time seemed to stand still.

"You had cancer," he said softly.

Tears welled up in my eyes as I stared at the blacktop driveway. My head bobbed up and down slightly and my breathing quickened.

"Life took on new meaning for you."

His words fed my soul.

"You followed your heart. I get it now. I'm really proud of you."

My head continued to bob up and down as I sobbed, "Thanks, Daddy. I love you, too."

Monday, October 11, 2010

Track season was over. Again. Punky, Mazey, and I had moved back into the house in Saratoga. Again. I started going to the gym regularly. I painted the living room, dining room, and hallway. I donated clothes that hadn't been worn in years. I invited friends for dinner. They usually brought food. I didn't spend much money. I walked in the park. I visited family. I rode my bike. I went to doctor appointments. I read books. I took pictures. I played with my cats. I went to the library. I pondered life. I consider working at Wal-Mart as a greeter or at Starbucks because they offered health insurance. I had options. I was alive. I didn't have cancer and I lived in America.

I thought back to when this whole thing had started with sitting on an exam table in search of a better life, in search of my next sex excursion. Most of my life had been wrapped around my need to have someone approve of me, have someone find me attractive, and have someone take care of me. I had spent forty years in search of a knight in shining armor, either in the form of a father-figure husband or a Crack-induced love affair. I'd supplemented my insanity with money, sales, business, growth opportunities, attractive titles, and networking events.

Maybe if I just sold another truckload of chairs. Maybe if I just took one more vacation. It was always a chase. It was always a longing, a desire, an outside search for acceptance and the need to fill that donut hole inside of me.

As I reflected on the last four, ten, twenty years of my life, I couldn't help but smile. If things had worked out like I had originally planned, my life would be full of cars, boats, men, real estate, and retirement accounts. Instead, I was close to broke—by American standards, anyway—a bit overweight, unemployed during an economic downturn, and totally single.

I was also full of love, compassion, and gratitude.

I guess it all worked out like it was supposed to.

Made in the USA
Middletown, DE
24 December 2019

81742755R10170